MADAM & EVE
All aboard for the Gravy Train

BY S. Francis, H. Dugmore & Rico

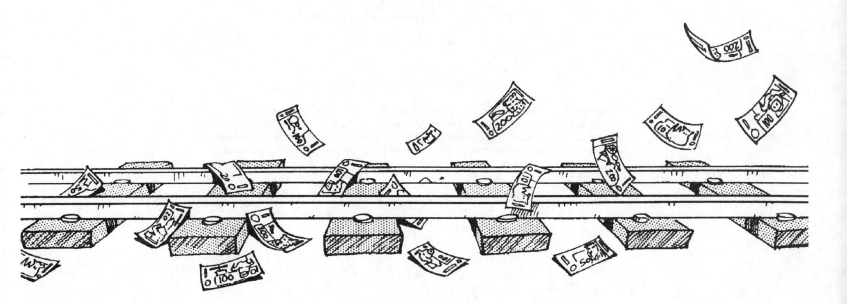

PENGUIN BOOKS

Published by the Penguin Group
27 Wrights Lane, London W8 5TZ, England
Viking Penguin, a division of Penguin Books USA Inc,
375 Hudson Street, New York, New York 10014, USA
Penguin Books Australia Ltd, Ringwood, Victoria, Australia
Penguin Books Canada Ltd, 10 Alcorn Avenue, Toronto, Ontario, Canada M4V 3B2
Penguin Books (NZ) Ltd, 182-190 Wairau Road, Auckland 10, New Zealand
Penguin Books, Amethyst Street, Theta Ext 1, Johannesburg, South Africa

Penguin Books Ltd, Registered Offices: Harmondsworth, Middlesex, England

First published by Penguin Books 1995

Copyright © S Francis, H Dugmore & R Schacherl 1995

ISBN 0 140 25652 0

Reproduction by Positive Proof cc
Printed and bound by Creda Press

MADAM&EVE

"FOR SHEER WIT AND SOPHISTICATED HUMOUR, THERE IS NOTHING IN SOUTH AFRICA TO TOUCH MADAM & EVE."
"… Can take its place alongside the world's best cartoon annuals – Giles, Andy Capp, Peanuts, Hagar."
– The EP Herald

"THE ANTICS OF MADAM & EVE HAVE THE COUNTRY IN STITCHES."
– South African News

"THESE TWO WOMEN HAVE CAPTURED A NEW NICHE IN POPULAR CULTURE."
– The New York Times

"MADAM & EVE … PROOF THAT SOUTH AFRICANS HAVE LEARNED TO LAUGH AT THEMSELVES."
– Newsweek

"HILARIOUSLY IRONIC …"
"… Acutely reflects the changes in modern South African society."
– The Big Issue, London

"TICKLES THE FUNNYBONE."
"Widely published and widely quoted."
– The Jerusalem Post

"OUTRAGEOUSLY FUNNY … WITH UNERRING HUMOUR AND INTELLIGENCE."
"If you haven't already fallen in love with Madam & Eve, this is a fine opportunity."
– Cosmopolitan Magazine

"THE MOST PAINLESS WAY OF UNDERSTANDING SOUTH AFRICAN POLITICS."
– The Guardian, London

"NOTHING HAS ESCAPED MADAM & EVE AND NOTHING WILL."
"Laugh out loud at the most up-to-date, audacious, scurrilous, politically correct, politically incorrect shrewd satire and judicious wit."
– Student Life Magazine

"DON'T MISS THIS ONE."
"Madam & Eve, almost national heroes by now, will have you rolling off your chair in laughter."
– The Natal Mercury

"THE MOST POPULAR CARTOON STRIP IN SOUTH AFRICA."
"… No one can ignore the infectious and telling humour."
– The Sunday Times

Other Madam & Eve Books

The Madam & Eve Collection
Madam & Eve, Free at Last

Madam & Eve appears regularly in:

The Mail & Guardian, The Star, The Saturday Star,
The Eastern Province Herald, The Natal Mercury,
The Natal Witness, The Cape Times, The Daily Dispatch,
The S.A. Times; Living, De Kat and Student Life Magazines.

8

...PLEASE? COME ON... JUST LET ME TRY **ONE** MORE TIME!

- SIGH. -

OKAY... NOW DON'T TELL ME! LET'S SEE... I GRAB YOUR HAND LIKE **THIS**...

...NOW HERE'S THE TRICKY PART. WAIT A MINUTE... HEY! I DID IT! **I DID IT!**

HILLARY! COME HERE! PRESIDENT MANDELA JUST TAUGHT ME THE AFRICAN HANDSHAKE!!

© Rapid Phase Entertainment —1996

AND TODAY'S TOP STORY... PRESIDENT MANDELA SPENT THE AFTERNOON WITH PRESIDENT CLINTON IN AN EFFORT TO RAISE MONEY FOR SOUTH AFRICA.

TELL ME, NELSON... WHY DO YOU KEEP WIPING YOUR EYES?

ACTUALLY BILL, IT'S FROM MY ROBBEN ISLAND DAYS...

YOU ROBBED ISLANDS?!!

NO **WONDER** YOU WENT TO PRISON! WHAT WERE YOU -- SOME KIND OF **PIRATE**?!

IS MY CHEQUE READY YET?

© Rapid Phase Entertainment —1996

AND, ACCORDING TO REPORTS, PRESIDENT MANDELA'S VISIT WITH U.S. PRESIDENT BILL CLINTON IS GOING EXTREMELY WELL.

SO TELL ME NELSON, WHY **EXACTLY** DO YOU NEED TO RAISE MONEY?

FOR RECONSTRUCTION AND DEVELOPMENT.

REALLY? MAYBE YOU SHOULD TALK TO MICHAEL JACKSON.

MICHAEL JACKSON?

YES, HE'S HAD **LOTS** OF RECONSTRUCTION AND DEVELOPMENT. ESPECIALLY ON HIS NOSE AND CHEEKBONES.

...COULD YOU SEE IF MY CHEQUE'S READY?

© Rapid Phase Entertainment —1996

MADAM & EVE

BY S. FRANCIS, H. DUGMORE & RICO.

AND IN OTHER NEWS, PAC GENERAL SECRETARY BENNY ALEXANDER HAS UNACCOUNTABLY CHANGED HIS NAME TO KHOISAN X.

I NEED TO GET TO THE BOTTOM OF THIS! I WANT THIS CLEARED UP IMMEDIATELY! GET ME KHOISAN X!!

YES, MR. PRESIDENT!

THE PRESIDENT WANTS TO GET TO THE BOTTOM OF THIS AND CLEAR THINGS UP. HE NEEDS KHOISAN X RIGHT AWAY.

I'LL TAKE CARE OF IT PERSONALLY!

QUICKLY! THE PRESIDENT WANTS TO GET TO THE BOTTOM OF THIS AND CLEAR THINGS UP! HE NEEDS KHOISAN X!

I'M ON MY WAY!

THE PRESIDENT NEEDS KHOISAN X!

...THE PRESIDENT NEEDS KHOISAN X!

CHEMIST

TO LET

THIS IS AN EMERGENCY! I NEED SOME KHOISAN X!!

DOES IT COME IN A TUBE OR A BOTTLE?

I DON'T KNOW! BUT THE PRESIDENT NEEDS SOMETHING TO CLEAR UP HIS BOTTOM!

-GASP- THE PRESIDENT?!!

...AND IN OTHER NEWS, RUMOURS PERSIST THAT PRESIDENT MANDELA IS SUFFERING FROM A SEVERE SKIN CONDITION AFFECTING HIS BUTTOCKS...

RING RING

GWEN! IT'S AFTER FIVE! WHERE'S MY GIN AND TONIC?!

MAYBE GIVING YOUR MOTHER A CELLULAR PHONE WASN'T SUCH A GOOD IDEA...

COME ON, YOU TWO! WHAT'S TAKING SO LONG IN THE KITCHEN?! WHERE'S MY GIN AND TONIC?!

I'VE JUST BEEN DE-CELLULARISED.

15

BY S. FRANCIS, H. DUGMORE & RICO

MY MAID EVE MADE ME COME TO THIS MEETING. SHE SAYS I CAN'T HELP MYSELF. THAT I ALWAYS BUY THOSE TV-ADVERTISED PRODUCTS.

AT FIRST, I STARTED SMALL. I ORDERED THE **NINJA STEAK KNIVES.** ...YOU KNOW THE ONES I MEAN -- THEY CUT THROUGH TIN CANS!

UH-HUH!

WE'VE ALL BEEN THERE!

AND SOON, I GAVE INTO **TEMPTATION.** I BOUGHT MORE... AND **MORE...** UNTIL I ORDERED THE MOST **EXPENSIVE** OF THEM ALL! THE DREADED... CHEF-O-MATIC!

GASP! GASP!

THAT'S RIGHT! THE **CHEF-O-MATIC!** IT SLICES! IT DICES! IT CUTS! IT CHOPS! ... THE ULTIMATE KITCHEN APPLIANCE!

THINK: AREN'T YOU **TIRED** OF **CRYING** EVERY TIME YOU CUT AN ONION?! WOULDN'T YOU LIKE TO SLICE TOMATOES **PERFECTLY?!**

YES!!

WELL, HOW MUCH WOULD YOU **PAY** FOR THIS **FABULOUS** KITCHEN HELPER?!

300 RAND!

TWO HUNDRED!

FOUR HUNDRED!

TWO-FIFTY!

BUT **WAIT!** DON'T ANSWER YET! IF YOU ACT **NOW,** YOU ALSO RECEIVE A COMPLETE SET OF DESSERT BOWLS... ALL FOR ONLY 99,99!

99,99?

I'VE GOT THE TOLL-FREE NUMBER! THERE'S A PAY-PHONE IN THE HALLWAY! **COME ON GIRLS!**

© Rapid Phase Entertainment — 1994

OOPS.

GOOD WORK, MADAM. THERE GOES MONTHS OF THERAPY DOWN THE DRAIN.

TV 1...
♫ THIS ONE'S FOR YOU! ♫

I'M CHIEF BUTHELEZI. I TRAINED HARD ... AND I CAN GO THE DISTANCE! AND NOW, I'M READY TO **KICK** SOME BUTT!

AND I'M PRINCE SIFISO ZULU. HE CAUGHT ME OFF-GUARD LAST TIME. BUT **THIS** TIME, I'LL BE **READY**!!

...THE REMATCH OF THE CENTURY! **LIVE!** THIS SUNDAY. ONLY ON ... **AGENDA!**

YAY!!

CHIEF BUTHELEZI?! YOU CAN'T GO IN THERE! WE'RE BROADCASTING!

WHERE'S MICHAEL J. FOX?!

SABC SAUK

MICHAEL J. FOX? THE ACTOR?

YES! I TAKE STRONG EXCEPTION TO HIS ACTING ABILITY! **WHERE IS HE?!**

UH, HE'S NOT HERE, SIR. "FAMILY TIES" IS PRODUCED IN AMERICA.

WELL, IF YOU SEE HIM, TELL HIM HE'S **HISTORY!**

COULD YOU PLEASE LEAVE NOW, SIR?

AND THAT SHOW "WHO'S THE **BOSS**"! TELL TONY DANZA HE'S A DEAD MAN!

AND NOW, AN EDITORIAL. TELEVISION STUDIOS -- IS NO ONE **SAFE**?! WE WILL **NOT** BE INTIMIDATED! WE WILL **NOT** --

...WHO'S THERE? WHO'S OUT THERE?!

EAT HOT LEAD, SCUMBUCKET!!

BLAM! BLAM! BLAM!

...SORRY ABOUT THAT. I'M JUST A LITTLE JUMPY. AND NOW, HERE'S THE WEATHER...

MADAM & EVE

BY S. FRANCIS, H. DUGMORE & RICO

OKAY, EVE... A LITTLE TO THE **RIGHT**! NOW THE LEFT! MORE TO THE **LEFT**!!

PERFECT! NOW HOLD IT!

M-NET. "WE WON'T STOP THE MAGIC."

:CLICK:

WHAT ARE YOU DOING? WE SHOULDN'T BE DOING THIS!

KISS ME, YOU FOOL!

... KISS ME LIKE YOU'VE NEVER KISSED ME BEFORE!

:SMACK! SMOOCH!:

NEIGHH! WHINNY!!
... CLOP CLOP CLOP CLOP CLOP!!

HOLY G#☆⚡!! WE FORGOT TO TIE UP THE HORSES!!

... AND WE'LL BE RIGHT BACK WITH MORE OF THE **PRINCESS DI** VIDEO AFTER THIS...

YES!!

©Rapid Phase Entertainment - 1994

AND IN OTHER NEWS, ONE OF THE CONTESTANTS FOR THE MISS SOUTH AFRICA PAGEANT HAS **DROPPED OUT** OF THE CONTEST...

A REPLACEMENT IS BEING SOUGHT IMMEDIATELY... FOR THE OPPORTUNITY TO WIN OVER **200,000 RANDS** IN **CASH** AND **MERCHANDISE**...

THIS IS **DEFINITELY NOT** PART OF MY JOB DESCRIPTION!

THIS WON'T WORK, MADAM! THEY'LL **NEVER** LET ME ENTER THE MISS SOUTH AFRICA PAGEANT!

YOU CAN DO IT, EVE.

ALL YOU NEED IS CHARM, POISE AND A WINNING PERSONALITY!

WE'VE GOT OUR WORK CUT OUT FOR US.

MAYBE WE CAN **BRIBE** A JUDGE.

WHAT DO YOU THINK, MOM?

NOT BAD. I THINK WE HAVE A SHOT AT THE PRIZE MONEY.

YOU'RE **WASTING** YOUR TIME, MADAM! I'LL NEVER **FOOL** THE JUDGES!

YOU DON'T HAVE TO **FOOL ANYONE**, EVE!

JUST BE YOUR-SELF! REMEMBER... BEAUTY PAGEANTS ARE ABOUT "CHARACTER"... "VALUES"... AND "INTEGRITY."

BY THE WAY, HERE'S YOUR I.D. YOUR NAME IS LIZEKA, YOU'RE 23... AND YOU JUST FINISHED UNIVERSITY.

MADAM & Eve

BY S. FRANCIS, H. DUGMORE & RICO

AAAAAH!!!

GEE... YOU'D THINK THEY NEVER SAW A PRESIDENTIAL BUST BEFORE.

I DON'T KNOW ABOUT YOU... BUT I CAN'T EAT MY CORNFLAKES WHILE NELSON MANDELA IS **STARING** AT ME.

I'M SORRY, EVE! BUT YOU CAN'T LEAVE THAT **HUGE** BUST OF THE PRESIDENT IN OUR KITCHEN!

MADAM-- THEY'RE **VERY** POPULAR! EVERYBODY'S BUYING THEM!

I'LL BUY YOU A SMALLER ONE! BUT THIS ONE HAS GOT TO GO!

BUT, MADAM-- YOU CAN'T JUST PUT IT OUT ON THE STREET! IT'S DIS-RESPECTFUL!

TRUST ME! I'LL SEND IT SOMEWHERE WHERE PEOPLE CAN ADMIRE IT EVERY DAY!

© Rapid Phase Entertainment - 1994

FOREIGNERS! THAT'S THE PROBLEM WITH THIS COUNTRY! EVERY DAY MORE AND MORE FOREIGNERS COME HERE AND NEVER LEAVE!

IT GET'S ME SO MAD, I COULD JUST... JUST...

GO BACK HOME TO ENGLAND?

EXACTLY!

AND, IN OTHER NEWS...

ACCORDING TO A RECENT SURVEY, A LARGE PERCENTAGE OF SOUTH AFRICANS SEEM TO BE SUFFERING FROM XENOPHOBIA.

WHAT'S "XENO-PHOBIA"?

FEAR OF NIGERIANS.

MOM!!

I'M TELLING YOU! ALL THE PROBLEMS IN THIS COUNTRY ARE CAUSED BY THE NIGERIAN CONSPIRACY!

"...NIGERIAN CONSPIRACY"?

MOM ALWAYS NEEDS A SCAPEGOAT. FIRST, IT WAS "ALIENS FROM OUTER SPACE". THEN IT WAS... "THE COMMUNISTS". NOW IT'S ..."THE NIGERIANS."

HMM. SHE COULD BE RIGHT! IN FACT... WHAT IF... THEY'RE ALL IN IT TOGETHER?!*

OF COURSE! ...NIGERIAN COMMUNISTS FROM OUTER SPACE!

DON'T YOU HAVE SOME IRONING TO DO?!

MADAM & EVE

BY S. FRANCIS, H. DUGMORE & RICO

AND, ACCORDING TO REPORTS, HUGE NUMBERS OF EX-MK SOLDIERS WHO RECENTLY JOINED THE SOUTH AFRICAN NATIONAL DEFENCE FORCE HAVE BEEN **IGNORING** ORDERS, **LEAVING** THEIR POSTS AND **GOING SHOPPING** WHENEVER THEY FEEL LIKE IT.

...DON'T GET ANY IDEAS.

ATTEN-SHUN!!

...YOU CALL YOURSELVES ...SOLDIERS?!!

YOU'RE NOTHING BUT A BUNCH OF ☆ⓖ#☆ MAGGOTS! I'VE SEEN ⓖ☆#☆ OLD LADIES MARCH BETTER THAN YOU DO!!

WELL I NEVER!

WHAT RUDE LANGUAGE!

I'VE NEVER HEARD ANYTHING LIKE THAT IN ALL MY LIFE!

I'VE **HAD** IT. LET'S GO SHOPPING.

GOOD IDEA.

WAIT A MINUTE! **HALT!** COME BACK HERE!! YOU CAN'T JUST **LEAVE!**

IF YOU ASK ME, LIEUTENANT... THIS ARMY'S IN **BIG** TROUBLE.

MAY I BE EXCUSED, SIR? MY DOG'S SICK.

HOW'S THE JOB HUNTING GOING, SOL?

IT'S **NOT** EASY, MRS. ANDERSON. I'VE BEEN LOOKING FOR A JOB IN MANAGEMENT... BUT YOU HAVE TO HAVE THE RIGHT **QUALIFICATION**.

WHAT QUALIFICATION IS THAT?

"SOWETO RESIDENT."

NO ONE'S ASKING YOU, MOM!

DON'T BE NERVOUS, SOL. I'M SURE YOU'LL GET THIS JOB.

AS LONG AS THEY HIRE ME ON **MERIT**... AND NOT BECAUSE OF AFFIRMATIVE ACTION.

CONGRATULATIONS! YOU'RE HIRED!

CONGRATULATIONS! YOU'RE HIRED!

I'M READY, NATALIE. SEND IN THE BLACK GUY.

GOOD LUCK WITH THE JOB INTERVIEW, SOL.

SIGH. THANKS.

HELLO... I'M...

CONGRATU-LATIONS!! YOU'RE HIRED!!

FORGET IT.

I WAS TOO QUICK, WASN'T I?

I'D AT LEAST WAIT FOR THE INTRODUCTION, SIR.

MADAM & EVE

BY S. FRANCIS, H. DUGMORE & RICO

SO THIS IS YOUR **NEW** OFFICE! WELL DONE, SOL!

THANKS, BUT LET'S FACE IT, THE **ONLY** REASON THEY HIRED ME IS BECAUSE OF **AFFIRMATIVE ACTION.**

WHAT MAKES YOU SAY THAT?

R&R CONSULTANTS

NOW FEATURING **2** BLACK EXECUTIVES

THIS COMPANY WAS DESPERATE TO HIRE **MORE** BLACK EXECUTIVES ...SO HERE I AM. I'VE **SOLD OUT**!

SOL, DON'T BE SO DEPRESSED. I'M SURE THEY HIRED YOU BECAUSE OF YOUR ENTHUSIASM, TALENT AND PREVIOUS EXPERIENCE.

...IN GARDENING?

SOL! PERFECT-- STAY RIGHT THERE!

OKAY EVERYONE! LET'S MOVE IT!

SMILE!

FLASH!

RIGHT. PUT IT ON THE PRESS RELEASE, ALL BUSINESS CARDS AND OUR CORPORATE LETTERHEAD!

...CORPORATE LETTER-HEAD?

I'D QUIT, BUT I ALREADY ACCEPTED THE BMW.

MADAM & EVE

SOUTH·AFRICAN·DEFENCE·EXHIBIT

CAN I HELP YOU?

NO THANKS. WE'RE JUST BROWSING.

LOOK AT THIS HELICOPTER, MADAM.

AH, YES! THE FX-37... GRIM REAPER -- THE MOTHER OF ALL ATTACK HELICOPTERS! EQUIPPED WITH SIX STINGER MISSILES. THIS BABY CAN TAKE OUT A WHOLE CITY BLOCK!

BUT... I'M JUST A DOMESTIC SERVANT.

NO PROBLEM!

CHECK THIS OUT! LOOKS LIKE AN ORDINARY VACUUM CLEANER, RIGHT?

BUT WAIT! -- I REMOVE THIS ATTACHMENT AND PUSH THIS BUTTON... AND...

VOILA! IT'S A **FLAMETHROWER**! WITH A KILL-ZONE OF 30 METRES, YOU'RE ABLE TO BURN AND SCORCH UNWELCOME VISITORS AT A MOMENT'S NOTICE. WE CALL IT THE VACU-TOASTER!

WE'LL HAVE TO THINK ABOUT IT.

EXCUSE ME...

WE'D LIKE TO **INVADE** A SMALL COUNTRY, BUT HAVE A LIMITED BUDGET.

NO PROBLEM! HEY JOE! BRING UP A NUMBER 103 WITHOUT THE NUKES!

LET'S GET OUT OF HERE!

LADIES... WAIT! WE HAVE A SPECIAL ON AK-47 KEY-RINGS!

© Rapid Phase Entertainment - 1994

43

MERRY CHRISTMAS! WE'RE ELVES! COME WITH US AND WE'LL GIVE YOU LOTS OF PRESENTS!

EVE!! THE TOKOLOSHES ARE BACK!!

TOLD YOU IT WOULD NEVER WORK.

HEY—IT WAS WORTH A TRY!

© Rapid Phase Entertainment – 1994

MADAM & Eve

BY S. FRANCIS, H. DUGMORE & RICO

HELP! THIS IS THE CAPTAIN OF THE ACHILLE LAURO! WE'RE SINKING! SOMEBODY HELP US! AAAAAGH!!

MOM! ARE YOU ALMOST FINISHED IN THE BATH?!

I'M RE-ENACTING THE DRAMA OF THE ACHILLE LAURO! I'LL BE OUT SOON.

SOME PEOPLE HAVE NO IMAGINATION.

GOOD NEWS, CAPTAIN! ALL THE PASSENGERS REACHED THE LIFEBOATS!

WE'RE SAFE! BUT WAIT! WHAT'S THAT IN THE WATER AHEAD?!

...A GIANT SHARK!! AAH! HELP! SWIM FOR LAND! IT'S OUR ONLY HOPE! SPLASH! SPLASH!

WE MADE IT CAPTAIN! WHAT A STRANGE ISLAND! IT APPEARS TO BE SQUARE!!

AND LOOK! WITH ALL THESE CHERRIES AND NUTS WE CAN SURVIVE FOR MONTHS!

MADAM... HAVE YOU SEEN THE CHRISTMAS FRUITCAKE?

MOM!! COME OUT OF THERE RIGHT NOW!! LOOK OUT! A GIANT TIDAL WAVE! SPLASH!

MADAM & Eve

BY S.FRANCIS, H.DUGMORE & RICO

MADAM & EVE PRESENT

A TRIBUTE TO GAUTENG

SOUTH AFRICA'S NEW PROVINCE

GAUTENG?!

BLESS YOU.

WE'LL HAVE THE GAUTENG DUCK PLEASE.

HOT AND SPICY OR REGULAR?

YOWWCH!!

GAUTENG!

GAUTENG!!

CAMPAIGN FOR A GUN-FREE SOUTH-AFRICA

MIELLLIES!!

GAUTENG!!

MALL

GAUTENG!!

GAUTENG!!

GAUGIN

VAN GOGH

GAUTENG

© Rapid Phase Entertainment – 1994

WAIT A MINUTE! YOU'RE TURNING "LONG WALK TO FREEDOM" INTO AN ACTION ADVENTURE COMEDY?

TRUST ME, MISTER PRESIDENT. POLITICS IS **NOT** GOOD BOX-OFFICE!

THAT'S WHY IN THE MOVIE VERSION, YOU'RE NO LONGER A POLITICAL PRISONER.

I'M NOT?

YOU'RE IN FOR ARMED ROBBERY.

WHAT?!!

DON'T WORRY! YOU'RE INNOCENT! YOU WERE FRAMED BY AN EX-CIA OPERATIVE WORKING FOR COLUMBIAN DRUG-LORDS!

THIS IS PREPOSTEROUS!! I **REFUSE** TO LET YOU TURN "LONG WALK TO FREEDOM" INTO ANOTHER **MINDLESS** ACTION-ADVENTURE FILM!!

THIS IS AN **IMPORTANT** STORY THAT MUST BE TOLD **TRUTHFULLY** WITHOUT GIMMICKS, CAR CHASES OR SPECIAL EFFECTS!!

...WE'LL GIVE YOU FIVE MILLION AND SEVEN PERCENT OF THE GROSS.

©Rapid Phase Entertainment - 1994

OF COURSE, "ESCAPE FROM ROBBEN ISLAND" IS A CATCHY TITLE.

WAIT!! I HAVEN'T EVEN TOLD YOU ABOUT THE DINOSAURS YET!

MADAM & EVE

BY S. FRANCIS, H. DUGMORE & RICO

THE HOLLYWOOD VERSION:

No jail could hold him.

No warder could break him.

No woman could tame him.

No bullet could stop him.

Wesley Snipes IS Nelson Mandela.

OKAY ERIC! SMILE!

SMILE?! HOW CAN I SMILE?! I HAVE NO FUTURE! NONE!

THERE'S NO JOBS OUT THERE! DO YOU HEAR ME?! IT'S HOPELESS!!

≈SOB≈ WHY DID I HAVE TO BE BORN WHITE?!

...GRADUATION JITTERS.

AS THIS YEAR'S FIRST GRADUATING CLASS IN THE NEW SOUTH AFRICA, I CONGRATULATE YOU.

FOR YOU, THIS IS A MOMENTOUS OCCASION. A TIME FOR NEW OPPORTUNITIES, PROSPERITY AND OPTIMISM AS YOU SEEK OUT CHALLENGING CAREERS.

THE FUTURE IS YOURS! EMBRACE IT WITH OPEN ARMS AS YOU FULFIL EACH AND EVERY ONE OF YOUR DREAMS! ...THANK YOU.

RIGHT. THAT COVERS THE BLACK GRADUATES. AND NOW, A BRIEF MESSAGE FOR ALL THE WHITE GRADUATES...

UH-OH.

AND I SAY TO OUR WHITE GRADUATES -- STOP BEING SO NEGATIVE AND PESSIMISTIC!

I'M SURE THERE'S SOMETHING IN YOUR FUTURE YOU CAN LOOK FORWARD TO! THINK ABOUT IT!

...YES? THE WHITE GRADUATE IN THE FOURTH ROW.

WELL, THE ROLLING STONES ARE COMING IN FEBRUARY.

SEE?! THERE YOU GO!

MADAM & EVE

BY S.FRANCIS, H.DUGMORE & RICO

ERIC! COME OUT OF THE BATHROOM RIGHT NOW!

I **CAN'T** DO THIS, MOM! I'M NOT **READY** TO FACE THE WORLD! I NEED MORE TIME!

EXACTLY HOW MUCH MORE TIME DO YOU NEED?

COUNTING POST-GRADUATE STUDIES, I FIGURE ANOTHER SIX YEARS.

WELL, LIZEKA-- THIS IS IT. GRADUATION DAY.

I KNOW. I CAN'T **WAIT** TO GET MY NEW BMW.

YOUR PARENTS ARE GIVING YOU A **BMW** FOR GRADUATION?!

NOT EXACTLY. I WAS JUST RECRUITED BY A BIG CORPORATION. IT'S PART OF MY EMPLOYMENT PACKAGE.

I CAN'T EVEN GET A JOB **INTERVIEW**-- AND YOU'VE ALREADY GOT A **BMW**!?

I GUESS BEING A BLACK FEMALE UNIVERSITY GRADUATE HAS IT'S ADVANTAGES...

IT'S NOT FAIR!! THE STRUGGLE WAS ALL ABOUT **EQUALITY!** HOW CAN I FEEL EQUAL WHEN YOU'RE DRIVING AROUND IN A NEW BMW!!

THEY GAVE YOU A CELLULAR PHONE TOO?!

TIC TIC TIC

HELLO, MISTER PIENAAR? IT'S LIZEKA. ABOUT THAT JOB I'M STARTING NEXT WEEK...

...I'LL BE NEEDING **TWO** BMW'S. ONE FOR ME AND ONE FOR MY FIANCÉ.

HE SAYS NO PROBLEM. FEEL BETTER NOW?

-GROAN-

MADAM & EVE

BY S. FRANCIS, H. DUGMORE & RICO

...AND NOW BACK TO "THE BOLD AND THE BEAUTIFUL".

AAAAH!

ERIC! WAS THAT YOU SCREAMING?!

IT'S OKAY, MOM. I JUST HAD A NIGHTMARE.

ERIC! DON'T YOU THINK IT'S TIME TO TAKE OFF THAT **GRADUATION OUTFIT**? YOU'VE BEEN WEARING IT NOW FOR **EIGHT WEEKS**!

WHY BOTHER, MOM? THERE'S NO JOBS OUT THERE ... **ZERO**!

BY WEARING THIS GRADUATION OUTFIT FOR **56 DAYS**, I'M ENGAGING IN NON-VIOLENT PROTEST OVER THE CURRENT JOB MARKET INEQUITY.

I AGREE., ALSO, IT MAKES THE WASHING AND IRONING A LOT **EASIER**.

YOU STAY OUT OF THIS!!

BESIDES, MOM. THERE'S **LOTS** OF **BENEFITS** TO WEARING A GRADUATION OUTFIT FOR 56 DAYS STRAIGHT.

NAME **ONE**!

RING! RING!

HELLO. ANDERSON RESIDENCE. HOLD ON ... I'LL GET HIM.

IT'S FOR YOU. THE GUINESS BOOK OF RECORDS.

I'M FAMOUS!

I'M RUBBER AND YOU'RE GLUE. EVERYTHING YOU SAY BOUNCES OFF ME AND STICKS TO YOU!

LIAR, LIAR PANTS ON FIRE!

THAT DOES IT! I QUIT!

GO AHEAD AND QUIT... CHICKEN!!

SHUT UP! NOBODY CALLS ME A CHICKEN!

MAKE ME! CLUCK! CLUCK! CLUCK! CLUCK!

AND WE'LL BE BACK WITH MORE OF THE MANDELA-DE KLERK SUMMIT AFTER THIS.

THANK YOU. YOU'RE FORGIVEN.

THANK YOU. YOU'RE FORGIVEN.

THANK YOU. YOU'RE FORGIVEN AND YOU'RE FORGIVEN.

INDEMNITY 20 RAND

LET ME GET THIS STRAIGHT. SOMEONE PAYS YOU MONEY AND THEN YOU FORGIVE THEM NO MATTER WHAT?!

THAT'S RIGHT.

INDEMNITY 20 RAND

HERE'S TWENTY BUCKS. I CHEATED ON MY GIRLFRIEND.

YOU'RE FORGIVEN.

INDEMNITY 20 RAND

BONK!

INDEMNITY 20 RAND

OF COURSE, SOMETIMES THERE'S PENANCE INVOLVED.

INDEMNITY 20 RAND

MADAM & EVE

BY S. FRANCIS, H. DUGMORE & RICO

GOOD AFTERNOON. SORRY TO TROUBLE YOU BUT I WAS WONDERING IF YOU'D LIKE TO CONTRIBUTE TO THE **ALLAN BOESAK** SECRET TRUST FUND.

A TRUST FUND? FOR WHAT?

SORRY. THAT'S A SECRET.

IN FACT, THE TRUST FUND IS **SO SECRET**, THAT THE PEOPLE WHO ARE SECRETLY AWARDED THE MONEY DON'T EVEN **KNOW** THEY'VE RECEIVED IT.

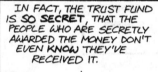

LOOK PAL, I AM NOT DONATING MONEY TO A TRUST FUND I KNOW NOTHING ABOUT!

HOW CAN YOU SAY THAT? YOU'RE ONE OF THE **TRUSTEES!**

WHAT?! ARE YOU CRAZY?! HOW CAN I BE A TRUSTEE?!

...YOU'RE A **SECRET** TRUSTEE!

RIGHT. THAT DOES IT! GET OUT OF MY HOUSE!

PLEASE! WE NEED THE MONEY! I HAVE A SECRET HOUSE, A SECRET WIFE AND THREE WONDERFULLY SECRET CHILDREN!!

FINE! LOOK-- HERE'S TEN BUCKS-- JUST GET OUT!

THANK YOU.

...JUST REMEMBER. I WAS NEVER HERE. YOU DON'T KNOW ME AND YOU NEVER GAVE ME ANY MONEY. NOW LET ME TEACH YOU THE SECRET HANDSHAKE.

WILL YOU PLEASE LEAVE?!

RIGHT. SHOULD I GO THROUGH THE FRONT DOOR OR IS THERE A SECRET ENTRANCE?

©Rapid Phase Entertainment - 1995

SOMEONE SHOULD PUT THE "TRUST" BACK IN TRUST FUND.

SLAM!!

60

MADAM & Eve

BY S.FRANCIS, H.DUGMORE & RICO

I HATE SECOND-HAND KNEE-HIGH SOCKS.

WELL, THANDI...THIS IS YOUR **FIRST DAY** AT YOUR **NEW** SCHOOL.

HAVE FUN.

HELLO.

WHY DON'T YOU JUST GO HOME?!!

YEAH! THIS WAS A GREAT SCHOOL UNTIL THEY HAD TO LET YOUR KIND IN!

UH-OH. HERE WE GO.

EXCUSE ME, BOYS... BUT I'LL HAVE YOU KNOW THIS IS THE **NEW SOUTH AFRICA!!** BLACK KIDS HAVE JUST AS MUCH A RIGHT TO BE HERE AS YOU DO!!

BLACK KIDS?!! WHO'S TALKING ABOUT BLACK KIDS?!!

THIS USED TO BE AN ALL-BOYS SCHOOL!

YEAH! AND GIRLS ARE YUCKY!!

YEAH!

WELL?! ARE YOU JUST GOING TO **STAND** THERE AND LET THEM GET AWAY WITH THAT ?!!

OUR GUEST TODAY IS THE **NEW** POLICE COMMISSIONER, GENERAL GEORGE FIVAZ.

GENERAL-- I UNDERSTAND YOU'RE ABOLISHING ALL **MILITARY** TITLES.

THAT'S RIGHT. I WANT TO MAKE THE POLICE SERVICE MORE **COMMUNITY-FRIENDLY**...

... AND BY THE WAY, PLEASE DON'T CALL ME "GENERAL."

ER, WHAT SHOULD WE CALL YOU?

"UNCLE GEORGE." THINK OF US AS **FRIENDLY** RELATIVES WITH GUNS.

POLICE COMMISSIONER FIVAZ...

PLEASE, CALL ME "UNCLE GEORGE." IT'S MORE COMMUNITY-FRIENDLY.

UNCLE GEORGE ... WHAT OTHER **CHANGES** ARE IN STORE FOR THE POLICE SERVICE?

A TOTAL IMAGE MAKEOVER. FROM NOW ON, I WANT PEOPLE TO THINK OF POLICE STATIONS AS **HAPPY, FRIENDLY** PLACES.

LIKE JOHN VORSTER SQUARE?

EXACTLY. WE'RE TURNING IT INTO A THEME PARK.

A **THEME PARK?!**

WE'RE CALLING IT... "DETENTION LAND" -- FUN FOR THE WHOLE FAMILY.

WE'RE BACK WITH THE NEW POLICE COMMISSIONER, GENERAL GEORGE FIVAZ, WHO INTENDS TO MAKE THE POLICE SERVICE MORE "**COMMUNITY-FRIENDLY**."

THAT'S RIGHT, JOHN.

COMMISSIONER-- SUPPOSE I'M A **SUSPECT** AND YOU'RE PURSUING ME. WHAT DO YOU DO?

WELL, WE NEVER SAY "FREEZE," JOHN. IT'S **NOT** COMMUNITY-FRIENDLY.

WHAT **DO** YOU SAY?

WE SHOUT "SMILE-- HAVE A HAPPY DAY... AND PLEASE STAND STILL!"

... AND IF I **DON'T**?

WELL, THEN WE BLOW YOU AWAY. BUT WE DO IT **NICELY**.

MADAM & Eve

BY S. FRANCIS, H. DUGMORE & RICO

AND COMING UP NEXT, WE'LL BE SHOWING A SPECIAL REPORT ON THE GROWING CORRUPTION IN THE NEW SOUTH AFRICA.

...OR MAYBE WE **WON'T** SHOW IT. WHAT'S IT **WORTH** TO YOU?

HELLO. I'M TAKING A GOVERNMENT SURVEY. DO YOU FEEL THERE'S TOO MUCH **CORRUPTION** IN THE NEW SOUTH AFRICA?

ARE YOU KIDDING?!

©Rapid Phase Entertainment · 1995

...SHADY TRUST FUNDS... BRIBERY...KICKBACKS... I'D HAVE TO SAY "YES."

WOULD TEN BUCKS **HELP** YOU CHANGE YOUR MIND?

POP!

GO AHEAD. TAKE THE MONEY.

NO. THAT WOULD BE WRONG. DON'T TAKE IT!

LISTEN TO HER, MADAM. IT'S A **BRIBE!** DON'T TAKE IT!

POP!

MIND YOUR OWN BUSINESS! SHE CAN TAKE IT IF SHE WANTS TO!

POP!

DON'T TAKE IT!

DON'T!

TAKE IT!

COULD YOU GIVE ME FIVE MINUTES? WE'RE HAVING A CAUCUS.

66

MADAM & Eve

BY S. FRANCIS, H. DUGMORE & RICO

I'VE HAD IT WITH YOU, YOU STUPID BLACK ⊙☆#☆!!

AND THAT GOES DOUBLE FOR ME YOU WHITE ⊙☆⊙#☆!!

CAR 54... INVESTIGATE REPORTS OF GUNFIRE...

THAT'S US.

RIGHT. LET'S GET TO WORK.

SCREEECH!!

OKAY, LET'S COVER THE ALLEY!

RIGHT. YOU GO FIRST.

NO WAY! YOU GO FIRST.

SO YOU CAN SHOOT ME IN THE BACK? FORGET IT!

OKAY, YOU IN THE ALLEY-- FREEZE!! WE'VE GOT YOU COVERED!

YOU FREEZE! WE'VE GOT YOU COVERED!

WHO'S THAT?

WE'RE THE POLICE, YOU ⊙☆#☆# DOGS!

WE'RE THE POLICE TOO, YOU STUPID ⊙☆#☆⊙☆!!

RIGHT. LET THE ⊙☆#⊙☆!! HAVE IT!

© Rapid Phase Entertainment - 1995

BLAM! BLAM!

BLAM TAKE THAT YOU ⊙☆#☆!!

BLAM BLAM

-OH YEAH!?

BLAM! BLAM!

...AND WE'LL BE BACK WITH MORE OF "HILLBROW STREET BLUES" AFTER THIS!

67

WINNIE... AS YOUR LAWYER, I'M TELLING YOU... YOU'RE IN BIG TROUBLE.

FIRST, YOU CRITICISE YOUR OWN GOVERNMENT... THEN YOU TRY AND PROMOTE YOUR DAUGHTER'S COMPANY...

...YOU CALL THE ROLLING STONES RACIST... AND THEN YOU SET UP THAT DUBIOUS VENTURE WITH OMAR SHARIF...

BUT I DIDN'T DO IT! I WAS IN BRANDFORT!

NICE TRY. WE USED THAT ONE ALREADY.

WINNIE... AS YOUR LAWYER ...I'M TELLING YOU -- YOU'RE IN BIG TROUBLE. YOU NEED SOME PLAUSIBLE DENIABILITY.

I DIDN'T DO IT! I WAS IN BRAND-FORT!

THEY'LL NEVER BUY IT. WE USED THAT ONE ALREADY.

OKAY. I'LL TELL YOU THE TRUTH.

...ALAN BOESAK MADE ME DO IT.

COULD WORK. I'LL MAKE SOME CALLS.

MICK!...MICK! WAKE UP!!

...WHA?

I JUST HEARD FROM SOUTH AFRICA! WINNIE MANDELA CALLED THE ROLLING STONES RACISTS BECAUSE WE'RE USING A WHITE PROMOTER!

WHOT?"

BUT THAT'S IMPOSSIBLE! YOU KNOW HOW MUCH I LOVE BLACK PEOPLE!

IT'S TRUE! HE REALLY DOES!

GO BACK TO SLEEP, LUV. I'LL HANDLE THIS.

MADAM & Eve

BY S. FRANCIS, H. DUGMORE & RICO

EVE! WAKE UP! WINNIE MANDELA JUST CRITICISED HER OWN GOVERNMENT, PROMOTED HER OWN DAUGHTER'S COMPANY, CALLED THE ROLLING STONES RACIST AND WENT INTO A DUBIOUS BUSINESS VENTURE WITH OMAR SHARIF.

ALL IN ONE DAY?!

TALK ABOUT SHOOTING HERSELF IN THE FOOT.

MUST HAVE BEEN AN AUTOMATIC WEAPON.

AT LEAST WINNIE STILL HAS QUITE A FEW SUPPORTERS.

SAVE WINNIE!

DON'T RESIGN!

I JUST HAD A THOUGHT, MADAM. WHAT IF WINNIE'S REALLY FORCED TO RESIGN?

I KNOW.

CAN YOU IMAGINE SOUTH AFRICAN POLITICS WITHOUT WINNIE MANDELA?

NO MORE SCANDALS!

NO MORE HILARIOUS MISTAKES!

NO MORE GOOFY GREEN HATS!

NO MORE BODYGUARDS!

NO MORE BITING SATIRE!

NO MORE GREAT PUNCHLINES!

SAVE WINNIE NOW

DON'T GO! WE NEED YOU!

© Rapid Phase Entertainment – 1995

MADAM & Eve

BY S. FRANCIS, H. DUGMORE & RICO

I CAN GET NO... I CAN GET NO... I CAN'T GET ME NO... NO SATISFACTION!!

HINT ALL YOU WANT. I'M NOT GETTING YOU ROLLING STONES TICKETS.

...TICKETS? YOU MEAN LIKE THESE? YOU BOUGHT TICKETS TO THE ROLLING STONES?!!

ACTUALLY... THEY'RE FREE. MICK SENT THEM TO ME.

MICK?!? ...MICK JAGGER?!!

DIDN'T I EVER TELL YOU? HE'S A PERSONAL FRIEND OF MINE.

HEE-HEE. SURE HE IS.

~ SIGH ~ MICK AND I MET A LONG TIME AGO. IT WAS A NIGHT I'LL NEVER FORGET. HE SAID I "INSPIRED" HIM.

OF COURSE... I WAS QUITE A PARTY ANIMAL IN THOSE DAYS.

RIGHT. WELL, WHEN YOU SEE HIM, TELL HIM I SAID HELLO.

TELL HIM YOURSELF. HE'S ON HIS WAY OVER HERE.

DING-DONG!

I'LL GET IT!!

© Rapid Phase Entertainment - 1995

MICK!

"BROWN SUGAR!"

MADAM & Eve

BY S. FRANCIS, H. DUGMORE & RICO.

HELLO. I WAS WONDERING IF YOU'D LIKE TO VOLUNTEER FOR OUR ANTI-CRIME BLOCKWATCH PROGRAM.

BLOCK-WATCH?

I HAVE MY HANDS FULL WITH MY OWN PROGRAM... MAIDWATCH!

OKAY. EVE...KEEP YOUR EYES PEELED FOR ANYONE SUSPICIOUS.

QUICK, MADAM! I JUST SAW A MAN WALKING DOWN THE STREET CARRYING A TELEVISION SET!

BLACK OR WHITE?

I THINK IT WAS A COLOUR TV·SET.

NO... I MEAN... WAS THE MAN BLACK... OR WHITE?

HE'S CARRYING A TV-SET! WHAT'S THE DIFFERENCE?!

WELL, IF HE'S BLACK, HE COULD BE A BURGLAR.

IF HE'S WHITE... HE COULD BE A TV-REPAIRMAN.

EXCUSE ME, SIR... WHAT ARE YOU DOING WITH THAT TV?

I'M A TV-REPAIR-MAN.

SEE?!

WHERE'S HIS TRUCK, MADAM?! AND BY THE WAY...

...THAT TV LOOKS EXACTLY LIKE OURS.

FREEZE!! HALT!! STOP THIEF!!

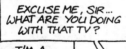

75

VOLUNTEER EVE SISULU REPORTING FOR **BLOCKWATCH** DUTY, CAPTAIN MADAM!

THAT'S THE SPIRIT, EVE. WE'VE GOT TO PROTECT THE NEIGHBOURHOOD FROM CRIME.

RIGHT. LET'S GO. HIT THE SIREN.

CLICK

...SOMEBODY STOLE IT.

WHERE TO, CAPTAIN MADAM?

NOWHERE. WE'RE JUST SUPPOSED TO DRIVE AROUND THE BLOCK FOR THREE HOURS.

ROGER, CAPTAIN MADAM, I COPY. TEN-FOUR. OVER AND OUT!

YOU'VE BEEN WATCHING NYPD BLUE AGAIN, HAVEN'T YOU?

AFFIRMATIVE.

:SIGH:

I'M SCANNING THE NEIGHBOURHOOD... AND SO FAR, ALL IS QUIET, CAPTAIN.

EVE, WE'RE **BLOCKWATCH** VOLUNTEERS... NOT NYPD BLUE COPS!

WAIT A MINUTE! WHAT'S THAT?! AN UPROOTED STOP SIGN.

I'M GOING IN! CALL FOR BACK-UP!

GET BACK IN HERE!!

STOP

77

HELLO...WINNIE?

YES?

HI. I JUST CALLED TO TELL YOU NOT TO GIVE UP! REMEMBER...YOU'RE INNOCENT UNTIL PROVEN GUILTY! GET YOURSELF A GOOD LAWYER!

AND BELIEVE ME... I KNOW WHAT IT'S LIKE TO BE PERSECUTED BY THE MEDIA. IT'S A RACIST CONSPIRACY! THEY WON'T REST UNTIL THEY--

...LET'S GO, OJ! THE TRIAL'S STARTING!

ONE MINUTE! I'M ON THE PHONE HERE!

I JUST HEARD FROM WINNIE, MISTER PRESIDENT.

...AND?

SHE SAYS SHE'S DONE NOTHING WRONG AND SHE'LL CONTINUE TO FIGHT THE DARK FORCES OF RACISTS AND CONSPIRATORS WHO PLOT HER DOWNFALL DAY AND NIGHT.

I DON'T BELIEVE IT! AM I NEVER GOING TO GET FREE OF THAT WOMAN?!

IT'S A LONG WALK TO FREEDOM, SIR.

OH, SHUT UP.

AND IN OTHER NEWS...

...WINNIE MANDELA DENIED ANY WRONGDOING AND CLAIMED PEOPLE WERE "OUT TO GET HER"...AND THAT SHE'S THE VICTIM OF A SECRET CONSPIRACY...

WHO'S WINNIE MANDELA AGAIN?

THE DEPUTY MINISTER OF ART, CULTURE AND SCIENCE FICTION.

MOM!!

MADAM & Eve

BY S.FRANCIS, H.DUGMORE & RICO

AND NOW WE CONTINUE WITH... "THE RAID ON WINNIE'S HOUSE..."

...BROUGHT TO YOU IN ELEVEN OFFICIAL LANGUAGES.

OKAY MEN! FAN OUT AND SEARCH FOR INCRIMINATING EVIDENCE! MOVE! MOVE! MOVE!

TROMP! TROMP! TROMP! TROMP!

CAPTAIN! I FOUND HER HAT!

NICE WORK, OFFICER. TAKE IT AWAY!

OKAY YOU. COME ALONG QUIETLY.

LOOK WHAT I FOUND, SIR. A ROLLING STONES POSTER WITH THE WORD "RACISTS" SCRAWLED OVER IT.

RIGHT. TAG IT AND BAG IT.

CHECK THIS OUT, SIR. TOWELS AND SOAP TAKEN FROM VARIOUS HOTELS.

WELL DONE. TAKE IT TO FORENSICS.

CAPTAIN! THE GUEST-BEDROOM! QUICKLY!

WHAT IS IT, SERGEANT?

THERE'S A MAN HIDING UNDER THE BED!

OKAY...YOU UNDER THE BED! ...IDENTIFY YOURSELF!

...DON'T SHOOT! I'M OMAR SHARIF!

RIGHT! PUT DOWN THAT MONEY AND COME OUT WITH YOUR HANDS UP!

81

AND IN OTHER NEWS, GOVERNMENT OFFICIALS WERE ONCE AGAIN CRITICIZED FOR THEIR BLOATED AND INFLATED SALARIES.

WHOO! WHOO! ALL ABOARD FOR THE GRAVY TRAIN!!

CHUGGA! CHUGGA!

REACTING IMMEDIATELY, PARLIAMENT TABLED A MOTION TO DRASTICALLY REDUCE ALL MONEY AND PERKS...

...THE MOTION WAS DEFEATED UNANIMOUSLY.

WHOO! WHOO! ALL ABBBOARD!

CHUGGA! CHUGGA!

IF I'VE TOLD YOU ONCE, I'VE TOLD YOU A THOUSAND TIMES...

WHEN YOU USE THE OVEN CLEANER OPEN ALL THE WINDOWS!

YAWN GOODNIGHT, EVE.

GOODNIGHT MOTHER ANDERSON.

BY THE WAY, I REALLY LIKE THOSE GREY FUZZY SLIPPERS.

WHAT GREY FUZZY SLIPPERS?

...I'VE REALLY GOT TO START DUSTING ON A MORE REGULAR BASIS.

85

MADAM & Eve

BY S FRANCIS, H. DUGMORE & RICO

WHIRRRRRR

BONK!

WHIRRRRRR

BONK!

WHIRRRRRR

THUMP!

MOM!

ARE YOU PUSHING THE ELECTRONIC GARAGE OPENER?!!

:CLICK:

WHEW...FOR A MOMENT THERE I THOUGHT THE TV REMOTE CONTROL WAS BROKEN.

MADAM & Eve

BY S.FRANCIS, H.DUGMORE & RICO

EXCUSE ME. COULD YOU LIFT YOUR FEET? WE'RE TRYING TO VACUUM.

THANK YOU.

RRRRRRRR...

DON'T LOOK NOW, EVE... BUT THE TOKOLOSHES ARE BACK.

I KNOW.

THEY APPEAR TO BE CLEANING THE LOUNGE.

I KNOW. I TOLD THEM TO.

YOU WHAT!?

HEY -- IT'S ABOUT TIME I HAD SOME HELP AROUND HERE!

WE'RE OUT OF OMO, MADAM.

THERE'S ANOTHER BOX IN THE KITCHEN.

© Rapid Phase Entertainment - 1995

THAT'S INCREDIBLE! WHAT'S IN IT FOR THEM?!

I PROMISED THEM I'D REMOVE THE BRICKS FROM UNDER YOUR BED!

WE'RE FINISHED WITH THE LOUNGE, MADAM.

RIGHT. START WASHING THE DISHES.

NOW HOLD ON JUST A DARN MINUTE!!

MADAM & Eve

BY S. FRANCIS, H. DUGMORE & RICO

AND NOW... BACK TO "EGOLI."

FACE IT, EVE. YOU CAN'T DO YOUR WORK AND WATCH SOAP OPERAS AT THE SAME TIME!

OF COURSE I CAN, MADAM--

...ALL I HAVE TO DO IS--

CLICK!

OOPS.

AOOAOOAOOAO

THAT WAS THE ARMED RESPONSE BUTTON--NOW YOU'RE IN BIG TROUBLE!!

FREEZE!!

SORRY GENTLEMEN. IT'S A FALSE ALARM--BECAUSE EVE'S TOO BUSY WATCHING SOAP OPERAS TO...

...IS ANYONE LISTENING TO ME ?!!

THIS IS HOPELESS.

CHIPS ?

MADAM & Eve

BY S. FRANCIS, H. DUGMORE & RICO

NO WORK NO FOOD NO CELLULAR TELEPHONE

RING RING

RING RING

RING RING

RING RING

YOU'RE KIDDING!

LET'S DO LUNCH...

ASK YOUR PEOPLE TO CALL MY PEOPLE...

AND THEN SHE SAID...

HELLO. MRS. PIENAAR? CAN CINDY COME OUT AND PLAY?

THAT DOES IT! I CAN'T TAKE IT ANYMORE! CELLULAR PHONES! THEY'RE EVERYWHERE, I TELL YOU!

TAKE IT EASY, MADAM. WHY DON'T WE GET SOME LUNCH?

OKAY. BUT IF I SEE OR HEAR ONE MORE CELLULAR PHONE...

WE'D LIKE A TABLE FOR TWO, PLEASE.

OF COURSE. WILL THAT BE CELLULAR OR NON-CELLULAR?

AAAAAH!!

WHAT'D I SAY?

91

MADAM & Eve

BY S. FRANCIS, H. DUGMORE & RICO

SEE ANY HAIRSTYLE ON THE COMPUTER YOU LIKE, MRS. ANDERSON?

NOT REALLY.

I KNOW WHAT YOU MEAN, MADAM. IT'S NOT **EASY** FINDING A STYLE THAT WORKS.

IT'S GOT TO BE ATTRACTIVE AND FASHIONABLE, YET COMFORTABLE AND EASY TO MANAGE.

MADAM... YOU WOULDN'T!

GO FOR IT!

CLIP!
CLIP!
CLIP!
CLIP!
SNIP!
SNIP!
SNIP!
SNIP!
BUZZ!!
CLIP
CLIP
CLIP

©Rapid Phase Entertainment – 1995

IT'S AMAZING HOW FAST THESE NEW STYLES CATCH ON.

IT'S DEFINITELY TIME TO CLEAN THE REFRIGERATOR.

WE ALL HAVE TO DO OUR PART TO HELP THE WATER SHORTAGE. FROM NOW ON, I'LL USE A WATERING CAN IN THE GARDEN INSTEAD OF A HOSE.

FROM NOW ON, I'LL TAKE A SHORT SHOWER INSTEAD OF A BATH.

FROM NOW ON, I'LL WASH THE DISHES ONLY ONCE A WEEK.

NICE TRY.

DARN.

VRRRRRRRR

SUCK!!

SSSSUCK!!

THAT'S WHY YOU DON'T SEE VERY MANY VACUUM CLEANERS IN CARTOON STRIPS.

MADAM & Eve

THE TWELVE DAYS OF CHRISTMAS

BY S. FRANCIS, H. DUGMORE & RICO

On the twelfth day of Christmas, my true love gave to me... twelve singers praising...

Eleven cellphones ringing...

Ten workers striking...

MORE PAY • ON RIKE • BET WAG

Nine squatters squatting...

Eight madams shopping...

Seven maids a-cleaning...

Six crates of beans and candles...

CANDLES

Five gold-en handshakes!

Four Parktown prawns...

Three French investors...

F F F

Two tons of silverware...

SPOONS • DESSERT BOWLS • SUGAR BOWLS • GRAVY BOATS • KNIVES

And a free house to give to Win-nie!

SOLD

MERRY CHRISTMAS!

Madam & Eve

MADAM & Eye

BY S. FRANCIS, H. DUGMORE & RICO

HI, ERIC ANDERSON. ARE YOU GUYS HERE FOR THE JOB INTERVIEW TOO?

THAT'S RIGHT.

WELL, GOOD LUCK. AND MAY THE BEST MAN WIN.

‹I LOVE OPTIMISM IN WHITE PEOPLE.›

GENTLEMEN... I'VE NARROWED MY CHOICE DOWN TO YOU TWO APPLICANTS. I WANT TO BE COMPLETELY FAIR AND HIRE THE MOST QUALIFIED CANDIDATE.

MR. MAHLABANE...IT SAYS ON YOUR CV THAT YOU WERE RECENTLY IN PRISON. WHEN WERE YOU PAROLED?

ACTUALLY, I WASN'T PAROLED. I WAS ONE OF 6800 CONVICTS WHO ESCAPED LAST YEAR.

YOU ESCAPED FROM PRISON?!

EXCELLENT! A SELF-STARTER WITH INITIATIVE! ...HOW DID YOU ESCAPE?

UH... I TIED BED SHEETS TOGETHER AND CLIMBED OUT OF A WINDOW.

STRATEGIC PLANNING AND PROBLEM SOLVING! MOST IMPRESSIVE!

BUT SIR... THIS MAN IS A WANTED CRIMINAL!

EXACTLY. AND THE FACT THAT HE'S AVOIDED CAPTURE SHOWS A BOLD COMPETITIVE EDGE!

I DON'T BELIEVE THIS.

WHAT WAS YOUR CRIME, SON?

UH... EMBEZZLEMENT.

PERFECT! AN INTIMATE KNOWLEDGE OF CREATIVE ACCOUNTING AND FINANCE!

GROAN

© Rapid Phase Entertainment - 1995

99

LET ME GET THIS STRAIGHT! 6800 PRISONERS ESCAPED FROM JAIL IN ONE YEAR?!

I'M AFRAID SO, SIR.

THIS IS OUTRAGEOUS! THESE PRISONERS MUST BE STOPPED!

I AGREE, SIR.

OKAY WARDEN! LET'S GO -- WE'RE GETTING OUT OF HERE!

ONE MINUTE! CAN'T YOU SEE I'M IN A MEETING?!

=MOAN= 6800 ESCAPED PRISONERS IN ONE YEAR! IS THIS POSSIBLE?!

I'M AFRAID SO, SIR.

... AND I'M GETTING OUT TOO! LET'S GO, WARDEN!

ARE YOU CRAZY!? YOU'RE A PRISON GUARD!

GIVE ME THAT GUN!

SORRY, SIR. IT'S CONTAGIOUS!

I LOVE MOVIE NIGHT AT THE PRISON.

NOT ONLY IS IT GOOD FOR MORALE... BUT IT KEEPS PRISONERS OCCUPIED.

WHAT ARE WE SHOWING TONIGHT?

IT'S A DOUBLE-FEATURE, "THE GREAT ESCAPE" AND "ESCAPE FROM ALCATRAZ."

...AGAIN?

THEY SEEM TO REALLY LIKE THEM, SIR.

MADAM & Eve

BY S. FRANCIS, H. DUGMORE & RICO

OPEN UP! IT'S THE POLICE!

EVE! THANK GOODNESS! THE POLICE ARE HERE!

THIS HAD BETTER BE GOOD.

YOU'RE WEARING... BATHROBES?!

HEY-- WE WERE RELAXING AT HOME.

NOW WHAT SEEMS TO BE THE PROBLEM?

SOMEBODY STOLE OUR TV-AERIAL.

I THOUGHT YOU SAID IT WAS AN EMERGENCY.

IT IS AN EMERGENCY-- LOVING STARTS IN ONE HOUR!

SIGH. OKAY. WE'LL NEED A DESCRIPTION OF THE PERPETRATOR.

WELL...HE SHOULDN'T BE TOO HARD TO SPOT. HE'S TALL... HE'S WEARING A MASK...

AND HE'S CARRYING A **HUGE TV AERIAL!!**

HMMM. THIS CALLS FOR A HIGH-SPEED PURSUIT.

RIGHT. THE NEXT BUS LEAVES IN 45 MINUTES.

BUS?!

YES... YOU DIDN'T THINK WE ACTUALLY DROVE HERE, DID YOU?

I HATE THIS POLICE GO-SLOW.

DID YOU BRING YOUR GUN?

NO, DID YOU?

MADAM & EVE

BY S. FRANCIS, H. DUGMORE & RICO

MISTER PRESIDENT... WE'VE PUT THIS OFF LONG ENOUGH! WE'VE GOT TO MAKE A DECISION ABOUT WINNIE'S FUTURE IN THE GOVERNMENT.

I AGREE. LET'S GET IT OVER WITH.

I SAY WE FLIP A COIN. WHO HAS ONE?

I DO!

I DO!

I DO!

I DO!

OKAY... THIS IS IT. HEADS, I FIRE HER. TAILS, SHE STAYS IN OFFICE.

FLIP!

CLINK! CLINK! SPIN! WOBBLE! CLINK!

OKAY... BEST OUT OF THREE.

GOOD IDEA, SIR.

FLIP!

CLINK! CLINK! SPIN! WOBBLE! CLINK!

DAMN! IS THIS WOMAN LUCKY OR WHAT?!

OKAY. WHERE WAS I? RIGHT. BEST OUT OF 127.

THIS IS THE ONE, SIR. I CAN FEEL IT.

© Rapid Phase Entertainment 1996

107

MADAM & Eve

BY S. FRANCIS, H. DUGMORE & RICO

WAKE UP EVERYBODY! I CAUGHT HIM! I CAUGHT THE EASTER BUNNY!!

KEEP THOSE PAWS WHERE I CAN SEE THEM!

PLEASE. I HAVE A FAMILY.

MOM! **WHAT** ARE YOU DOING?! PUT DOWN THAT WATER PISTOL! YOU CAN'T **ARREST**... YOU CAN'T ARREST...

YOU'RE THE EASTER BUNNY?!

NOT EXACTLY. I'M THE **EASTER DASSIE**.

THE EASTER DASSIE???

THE EASTER BUNNY TOOK A VOLUNTARY RETRENCHMENT PACKAGE.

...HE WAS CONSIDERED TOO EUROCENTRIC. I'M AN AFFIRMATIVE ACTION APPOINTMENT.

AFFIRMATIVE ACTION?

IT'S NOT A BAD JOB, EITHER. I GET A GREAT SALARY, AN OFFICIAL TITLE, A BMW... AND I ONLY HAVE TO SHOW UP FOR WORK **ONCE** A YEAR.

WHAT'S YOUR OFFICIAL TITLE?

DEPUTY MINISTER OF EASTER EGGS, BASKETS AND CHOCOLATE.

OF COURSE, I WAS HOPING TO GET THE **TOOTH FAIRY** POSTING, BUT I HAD NO FINANCIAL EXPERIENCE.

I'M GOING BACK TO BED. MAYBE THIS IS ALL A DREAM.

HEY! DON'T YOU WANT YOUR CHOCOLATE DASSIE?!

MADAM & EVE

BY S.FRANCIS, H. DUGMORE & RICO

TODAY'S TOP STORY...
BY UNCOVERING YET ANOTHER LOOPHOLE, WINNIE MANDELA WAS FIRED AND REHIRED FOR THE 47th TIME THIS WEEK.

AAAAAHH!! WE'LL GET HER NEXT TIME, SIR. I PROMISE.

OKAY. LET'S TRY THIS AGAIN... AND THIS TIME, NO MORE STUPID MISTAKES.

YES, MISTER PRESIDENT.

DID WE USE BLACK INK AND IS THE DOCUMENT TYPEWRITTEN?

YES, SIR.

ARE ALL THE i's DOTTED AND ALL THE t's CROSSED?

YES, SIR.

DID WE USE WHITE PAPER INSTEAD OF PINK OR YELLOW?

YES, SIR.

WAIT A MINUTE! WHAT ABOUT AN OFFICIAL SEAL FOR THE LETTER?

RIGHT HERE, SIR.

URK! URK!

GOOD. THEN WE'VE THOUGHT OF EVERYTHING.

GO! ...FIND WINNIE!

URK! URK!

AND NOW, TONIGHT'S PROGRAMME LINE-UP. FIRST, THE POPULAR INTERVIEW SHOW "HIDDEN AGENDA."

FOLLOWED BY PART ONE OF THE EXCITING MINISERIES "LONG WALK TO FREEDOM."

AND FINALLY, OUR MOVIE TONIGHT IS "BOESAK" – THE STORY OF AN INNOCENT MAN FIGHTING TO CLEAR HIS NAME.

AND WE'LL BE RIGHT BACK WITH THE ANC CHANNEL AFTER THIS...

AND NOW FOR TODAY'S WEATHER... WARM, BEAUTIFUL DAYS AHEAD, THANKS TO THE RDP AND FREE MEALS FOR SCHOOL-GOING CHILDREN.

A TEMPORARY COLD FRONT IS EXPECTED... BUT THAT'S NO PROBLEM, SINCE WE'RE BUILDING OVER ONE MILLION NEW HOUSES.

... AND FINALLY, SOME LIGHT DRIZZLE DUE TO THE NATIONAL PARTY'S INABILITY TO REALISE THAT THEY LOST THE LAST ELECTION.

THIS IS THE ANC CHANNEL. THANK YOU FOR WATCHING.

JOHN! MY ILLEGITIMATE HALF-BROTHER WHO WE THOUGHT WAS KILLED IN A SKIING ACCIDENT! AFTER ALL THESE YEARS, YOU'VE COME BACK.

YES, MARY. I'VE HAD PLASTIC SURGERY.

THIS IS WONDERFUL, JOHN! NOW, WE CAN WORK FOR THE RDP TOGETHER!

I'M SORRY, MARY. YOU SEE, I'VE CHANGED. I NO LONGER CARE ABOUT THE GOVERNMENT OF NATIONAL UNITY.

YOU MEAN...

YES. ...I'M A POPULIST NOW!

GASP!

THIS IS THE ANC CHANNEL. STAY TUNED FOR MORE OF THE "BOLD AND THE DUTIFUL" AFTER THIS.

WELCOME TO THE **ANC CHANNEL**. TONIGHT'S MOVIE IS "MANDELA."

THIS IS THE **INKATHA FREEDOM PARTY** CHANNEL. TONIGHT'S MOVIE IS "SHAKA ZULU."

...AND TONIGHT ON THE **DEMOCRATIC PARTY** CHANNEL, WE PRESENT "CRY FREEDOM".

THIS IS THE **SOCCER PARTY** CHANNEL. STAY TUNED FOR "ONE FLEW OVER THE CUCKOO'S NEST."

AND IN OTHER NEWS, THE PRESIDENT CRITICISED POLITICIANS WHO *EAT* FROM THE *TROUGH*...

...WHO **BUTTER** THEIR **BREAD** ON BOTH SIDES AND TAKE ADVANTAGE OF THE **GRAVY** TRAIN.

HE HOPES TO **BEEF** UP THE BUDGET, SO MORE SOUTH AFRICANS CAN BRING HOME THE BACON...

EVE! WHEN'S DINNER?! I'M GETTING **HUNGRY!!**

MADAM & Eve

BY S. FRANCIS, H. DUGMORE & RICO

ERIC?!

VUSI!! I HAVEN'T SEEN YOU SINCE WE TOOK OVER THE ADMINISTRATION BUILDING IN HIGH SCHOOL!!

THOSE WERE THE DAYS, MY FRIEND.

=SIGH= WE THOUGHT THEY'D NEVER END.

YOU KNOW, VUSI — YOU WERE THE **BEST** SOCCER PLAYER I EVER SAW. ARE YOU STILL ACTIVE IN SPORT?

NO — BUT I'M GETTING MARRIED SOON.

CONGRATULATIONS!

AND YOU'RE NOT GOING TO BELIEVE THIS. IT'S A **NON-RACIAL** RELATIONSHIP.

REALLY?! **I'M** INVOLVED IN A NON-RACIAL RELATIONSHIP TOO!

NO KIDDING! DO PEOPLE STARE AT YOU IN PUBLIC?

ALL THE TIME! PEOPLE ARE SO CLOSE-MINDED!

YOU CAN SAY THAT AGAIN.

DON'T LET IT BOTHER YOU. I SAY, IF TWO PEOPLE **LOVE** EACH OTHER, THAT'S ALL THAT MATTERS.

MAYBE I COULD **MEET** YOUR FIANCE SOMETIME.

THAT'S NO PROBLEM! HERE HE COMES NOW!

FRANK — SAY HELLO TO ERIC.

HI!

ERIC'S IN A NON-RACIAL RELATIONSHIP TOO.

REALLY? ANYONE WE KNOW?

BILL PLEASE!

MADAM & Eve
BY S. FRANCIS, H. DUGMORE & RICO

IT'S **HOPELESS**! I WAS UP ALL LAST NIGHT AND I'LL NEVER PASS MY **ENGLISH LITERATURE** CLASS ON SHAKESPEARE!

POP!

BE NOT AFRAID. STUDY HARD AND TO THY OWN SELF BE TRUE.

POOF!

...I'VE DEFINITELY GOT TO STOP TAKING THOSE **CAFFEINE** PILLS.

MAYBE ONE OF EVE'S NICE DINNERS WILL CALM ME DOWN.

MOM? EVE?! I'M HOME FROM UNIVERSITY!

HARK! WHAT LIGHT THROUGH YONDER DOOR BREAKS?

AAAAAH!!

YOU'D THINK HE NEVER SAW SOMEBODY GO TO A **FANCY DRESS** PARTY BEFORE.

MADAM & Eve

BY S. FRANCIS, H. DUGMORE & RICO.

YOU'RE LATE! PULL UP A CHAIR!

SORRY MISTER PRESIDENT.

COMING THROUGH!

BONK!

BONK!

BONK!

OUCH!

OW!

MAYBE YOU BETTER STAND.

YES SIR.

LET'S GET DOWN TO BUSINESS. I'M VERY UNHAPPY WITH THE WAY WE'VE BEEN HANDLING THINGS IN SUCH A CLUMSY MANNER.

FIRST WE TRIPPED OVER WINNIE'S SEARCH WARRANT AND DISMISSAL... AND THEN WE FUMBLED THE ALLAN BOESAK INVESTIGATION.

IT WASN'T OUR FAULT, SIR...

WE TRIED TO BE CAREFUL!

SMACK!

OOPS.

AAAAAAAAAAAA!

OKAY. I'M GIVING YOU ONE MORE CHANCE. AND THIS TIME, NO MORE MISTAKES!

RIGHT, SIR. YOU CAN COUNT ON US.

SLAM!

CRASH!

CLATTER!

CLANG!

...THAT'S THE BROOM CUPBOARD.

YES, SIR. WE SEE THAT NOW.

SO *THIS* IS WORLD CUP RUGBY. A BUNCH OF *GROWN MEN* FIGHTING OVER A BALL. WHAT'S SO *EXCITING* ABOUT THAT?!

COME ON! GET THAT ⑥☆#⑥ BALL! JUMP ON HIS ☆⑥#☆ HEAD!!

© Rapid Pace Entertainment - 1995

AND WE'LL BE BACK TO MORE *WORLD CUP RUGBY* AFTER THIS...

EVE! YOU FORGOT THE LEMON FOR MY GIN & TONIC!

HERE YOU GO.

– PUNT!

WORLD CUP FEVER. IT'S CONTAGIOUS.

OKAY. LET'S TRY IT AGAIN. NEW ZEALAND ARE THE ALL BLACKS.

EXCEPT THEY'RE ALL WHITE.

THEY'RE NOT ALL WHITE. SOME OF THEM ARE BLACK.

SO THE ALL BLACKS ARE NOT ALL WHITE.

RIGHT.

BUT THEY'RE NOT ALL BLACKS, EITHER.

YOU'RE DOING THIS ON PURPOSE, AREN'T YOU?!

© Rapid Pace Entertainment - 1995

124

POP!

HELP! I'M SURROUNDED BY THIRTY BIG SWEATY MEN!

WHOOPEE!!

WAKE UP, MOM! YOU'RE MISSING AN EXCITING RUGBY MATCH!

HUH? ..WHAT?

〈LOOK EVERYONE! IT'S THE RUGBY WORLD CUP MASCOT!〉

HALO!

BONJOUR!

HELLO!

〈OKAY, GUYS! LET'S HIT THE SHOWERS!〉

YES! BEEFCAKE CITY!

I CAN'T BELIEVE YOU TALKED ME INTO THIS!

...AND IT'S ANOTHER TRY FOR THE SPRINGBOKS!!

EVE -- I DIDN'T KNOW BLACK PEOPLE LIKED RUGBY.

OH YES, MADAM. IT'S VERY EXCITING.

ALSO, IT'S NOT EVERY DAY WE GET TO SEE THIRTY WHITE GUYS BEAT EACH OTHER SENSELESS.

MADAM & Eve

BY S. FRANCIS, H. DUGMORE & RICO

BUENOS DIAS. GOOD MORNING.

FLASH!!

ARE YOU READY TO ORDER?

YES, WE'D LIKE THE BACON AND EGGS WITH DRY TOAST.

TWO #3 BREAKFAST SPECIALS— HOLD THE BUTTER!

COMING UP!

EXCUSE ME ...BUT COULD SOMEONE PLEASE TELL ME...

...JUST WHAT THE HECK IS GOING ON AROUND HERE ?!!

EVE & ANDERSON'S WORLD-CUP BED & BREAKFAST ALL RUGBY FANS WELCOME!

MADAM & EVE

BY S. FRANCIS, H. DUGMORE & RICO

IS IT SERIOUS, DOCTOR?

I'M AFRAID SO, MRS. ANDERSON.

YOUR MOTHER HAS WORLD CUP FEVER.

DON'T DROP THE @#☆@ BALL YOU MORON!!

I'M AFRAID THE SYMPTOMS ARE UNMISTAKABLE... INABILITY TO TURN OFF THE TV... A CRAVING FOR JUNK FOOD AND ALCOHOL... SUDDEN VIOLENT OUTBURSTS...

HOW LONG DOES IT LAST, DOCTOR?

ABOUT SIX WEEKS INCLUDING THE FINALS.

FORWARD PASS!! THAT WAS A @☆#@ FORWARD PASS!!

QUICK! SHE'S HAVING A SEIZURE!

CAN YOU BELIEVE THAT @☆#@ REF ALLOWED THAT TRY?!!

HOLD HER DOWN. IT'LL PASS.

CAN SHE HEAR ME, DOCTOR?

NOT NOW. BUT SOMETIMES THE FEVER UNEXPLAINABLY BREAKS FOR A SHORT DURATION.

...AND WE'LL BE RIGHT BACK WITH MORE WORLD CUP RUGBY AFTER HALF-TIME.

...GWEN? IS THAT YOU?

...MOM?

GWEN!

MOM! YOU'VE COME BACK TO ME!!

HURRY. YOU ONLY HAVE ABOUT 15 MINUTES.

© Rapid Phase Entertainment - 1995

MADAM & Eve

BY S.FRANCIS, H.DUGMORE & RICO

IT'S JUST **TOO MUCH** TO TAKE, DOCTOR. THE CONSTANT PRESSURE... THE SLEEPLESS NIGHTS... THE FEAR OF FAILURE...

I UNDERSTAND, MRS. ANDERSON. HOW LONG HAVE YOU FELT THIS WAY?

NOT ME! THE **SPRINGBOKS**!! WHAT IF THEY DON'T MAKE THE **FINALS**?!

WHEN DID YOU FIRST BECOME AWARE OF THESE... SYMPTOMS, MRS. ANDERSON?

AT THE OPENING GAME! A FRIEND OF MINE SAID "GO AHEAD -- TURN ON THE TV AND GIVE IT A TRY." IT WAS **PEER PRESSURE!**

NEXT THING I KNEW, I WAS **HOOKED!** I HAD TO WATCH **EVERY GAME!** I EVEN CRUISED THE STREETS LOOKING TO BUY **BLACK MARKET TICKETS!**

AFTER THAT, IT GOT WORSE. LAST WEEK, EVE CAUGHT ME IN FRONT OF THE MAKE-UP MIRROR...

I WAS PAINTING A **SOUTH AFRICAN FLAG** ON MY FACE! ≈CHOKE≈

I SEE.

AND THAT'S NOT ALL! YESTERDAY I EVEN BOUGHT A **SPRINGBOK JERSEY** AND A PAIR OF **RUGBY BOOTS**!!

YOU MEAN...

YES! I CAN'T HELP MYSELF! I'VE TURNED INTO... INTO...

A RUGBY FANATIC!!

OW! GET A GRIP, MRS. ANDERSON! YOU'RE STANDING ON MY KNEE!

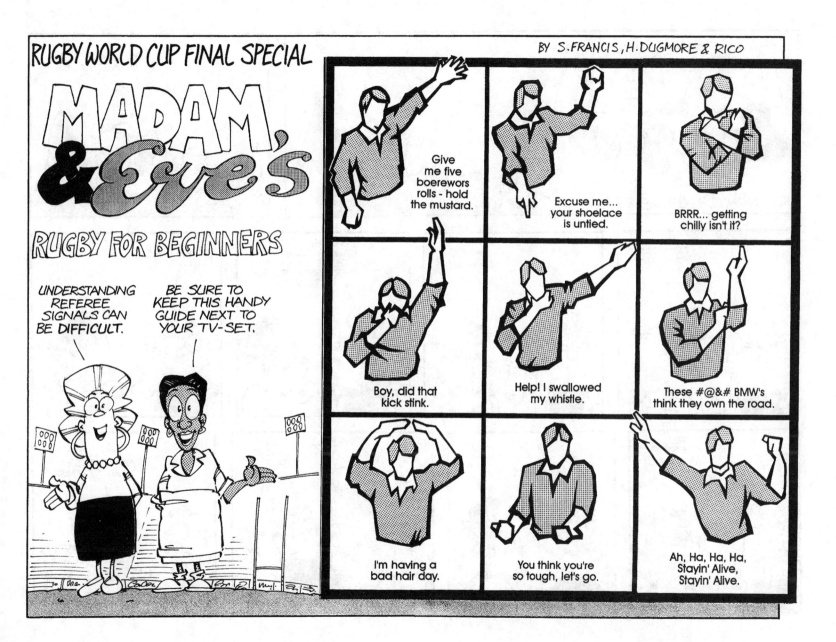

MADAM & Eve

BY S. FRANCIS, H. DUGMORE & RICO.

MY WORLD CUP RUNNETH OVER.

TO FRANCOIS PIENAAR!

TO JAMES SMALL!

MADAM... HOW MANY PLAYERS ARE THERE IN THE SPRINGBOK RUGBY SQUAD?

TWENTY-SIX, ...WHY?

TO CHESTER WILLIAMS!

TO ANDRE JOUBERT.

...AND LET'S NOT FORGET JOEL STRANSKY!

DIAGNOSIS: A SEVERE CASE OF *RUGBY DEPRIVATION PSYCHOSIS*, DUE TO A SUDDEN ABSENCE OF RUGBY TELEVISION BROADCASTS. PATIENT SEEMS CATATONIC... AND DOES NOT RESPOND TO OUTSIDE STIMULI.

THEREFORE, I AM ABOUT TO ATTEMPT A RADICAL TYPE OF NEW THERAPY.

LOOK. A RUGBY BALL.

AAAARGH! CRASH! HELP! SHE'S TACKLING ME!

TELL ME, DOCTOR... IS THERE ANY HOPE FOR MY MOTHER?

SORRY, MRS. ANDERSON. RUGBY DEPRIVATION PSYCHOSIS IS VERY SERIOUS. SHE COULD REMAIN LIKE THIS FOR SOME TIME.

IN MY OPINION, THIS WILL REQUIRE LONG HOURS OF THERAPY AND COST *THOUSANDS* OF RANDS.

G...GWEN? ...IS THAT YOU?

MOM! YOU'VE COME BACK TO US!

IT'S A MIRACLE.

WELL... THAT'S ANOTHER GONE.

ONLY 1421 DAYS LEFT!

COUNTDOWN TO THE NEXT RUGBY WORLD CUP.

© Rapid Phase Entertainment - 1995

WHAT A DAY FOR SPORT AND POLITICS! THE ANC AND THE IFP HAVE DECIDED TO RESOLVE THEIR DIFFERENCES WITH A GAME OF RUGBY!

AND HERE COMES THE ANC TEAM LED BY CAPTAIN MANDELA!

AND HERE COMES THE IFP TEAM LED BY CAPTAIN BUTHELEZI!

WAIT A MINUTE! THERE'S SOME COMMOTION ON THE FIELD! THE IFP ARE MOVING THE GOALPOSTS!

THE ANC-IFP RUGBY GAME IS ABOUT TO BEGIN! TEAM CAPTAINS MANDELA AND BUTHELEZI ARE IN THE CENTRE OF THE FIELD FOR THE COIN TOSS...

AND ALLAN BOESAK HAS JUST FLIPPED THE COIN!

THAT'S STRANGE. THE COIN SEEMS TO HAVE GONE MISSING.

WHAT A TEST, LADIES AND GENTLEMEN -- THE ULTIMATE RUGBY GAME BETWEEN THE ANC AND THE IFP!

AND THERE'S A GOOD DROP-KICK BY MANDELA! IT LOOKS LIKE HE'S GOING TO SCORE!

PUNT!

PFFF!

THUNK!!

WHOA!! THAT DOES IT! THE REFEREE IS CONFISCATING ALL CULTURAL WEAPONS!!

AND WE CONTINUE WITH THE "WINNER-TAKE-ALL" **RUGBY** MATCH BETWEEN THE ANC AND THE IFP...

THE ANC HAS POSSESSION... AND THERE'S THE PASS-- IT'S OVER TO MANDELA!

MANDELA PASSES TO SEXWALE... SEXWALE PASSES TO RAMAPHOSA-- AND NOW IT'S THABO M'BEKI! LOOK AT HIM GO!

WAIT, THABO! COME BACK! YOU'RE RUNNING THE WRONG WAY!!

AND THE ANC HAS SCORED THE FIRST TRY IN THIS EXCITING ANC-IFP **RUGBY MATCH**! BUT WAIT--THE IFP IS CLAIMING AN ILLEGAL FORWARD PASS!

IFP CAPTAIN BUTHELEZI IS DEMANDING INTERNATIONAL MEDIATION... AND HERE COMES HENRY KISSINGER!

JA, I HAF TO AGREE. DIS VAS DEFINITELY A FORWARD PASS.

WHOA!! TOUGH BREAK FOR THE ANC.

AND HERE IT IS, LADIES AND GENTLEMEN. THE FINAL ANC-IFP RUGBY MATCH TO SETTLE THEIR DIFFERENCES...

THE GAME IS ABOUT TO START...

WAIT A MINUTE -- THERE SEEMS TO BE SOME COMMOTION DOWN ON THE RUGBY FIELD...

NOBODY ON THE ANC TEAM WANTS TO PLAY ON THE "RIGHT WING!"

ERIC--I WANT YOU TO HAVE A TALK WITH MY FOURTEEN YEAR-OLD COUSIN VUSI.

THE GOVERNMENT JUST RELEASED HIM FROM PRISON. HE'S AN INCORRIGIBLE THIEF.

INCORRIGIBLE? COME ON LIZEKA... NOBODY'S INCORRIGIBLE.

HEY MAN, HOW ABOUT YOU AND ME HAVE A LITTLE RAP?

GOOD. BUT BEFORE YOU START, TELL HIM TO GIVE YOU YOUR WALLET BACK.

DIDN'T FEEL A THING, DID YOU?

VUSI... YOU'RE ONLY FOURTEEN. YOU'VE GOT TO STOP STEALING!

I CAN'T HELP IT, MAN. THERE'S A HUGE RESALE MARKET FOR STOLEN MERCHANDISE.

...AND CARS! I MEAN, TELL THE TRUTH... ISN'T THERE A CAR OUT THERE YOU'VE ALWAYS WANTED?

WELL ... I'VE ALWAYS BEEN PARTIAL TO A BMW 325 CONVERTIBLE.

NO PROBLEM, MAN. WHAT COLOUR?

ERIC! YOU'RE SUPPOSED TO BE HELPING HIM!

SO YOU SEE, VUSI... IF I ACCEPTED A STOLEN BMW, I'M JUST AS GUILTY AS THE PERSON WHO STOLE IT.

BESIDES, I ALREADY HAVE A NICE VOLKS-WAGEN I'M VERY HAPPY WITH.

THE GREEN GOLF PARKED OUT IN FRONT?! DON'T TELL ME THAT'S YOURS?!

...YOU DIDN'T.

TAP TAP TAP TAP TAP

HEY! MY CAR'S GONE!

SELO? IT'S VUSI. BRING IT BACK. WE MADE A MISTAKE.

142

CADET XYBORG CALLING MARS. WE ARE PREPARING TO INITIATE SECRET UNDERGROUND LANDING.

BZZZZZZZZ

HMMMMM

MISSION SUCCESSFUL. EARTHLINGS COMPLETELY UNAWARE OF OUR PRESENCE. WHEN ENTIRE FLEET HAS LANDED, WE WILL COMMENCE INVASION OF EARTH... XYBORG OUT.

GOODNIGHT XYBORG.

GOODNIGHT ZORG.

SCREECH!!

ANOTHER TRAFFIC CIRCLE ON OUR STREET?!

IT'S AMAZING HOW THESE THINGS JUST SPRING UP OVERNIGHT.

SLAM! I'M BACK FROM THE MOVIE THEATRE, MADAM.

HOW WAS IT?

THE USUAL. COPS, ROBBERS, HIJACKINGS AND CAR CRASHES.

SOUNDS LIKE A VIOLENT MOVIE.

MOVIE?

THAT WAS JUST THE TAXI RIDE TO GET THERE.

MADAM! WHAT HAPPENED TO THE BURGLAR BARS?!

I HAD THEM REMOVED!

REMOVED?!

YES. I FELT LIKE A PRISONER IN MY OWN HOUSE.

NOW WE CAN LEAN OUT OF THE WINDOW AND FEEL THE SUNSHINE... AND SMELL THE AIR. TRY IT!

GO AHEAD -- ENJOY THE VIEW.

SEE EVE? IT'S EASY TO LEARN CHESS. JUST THINK IN TERMS OF SOUTH AFRICAN POLITICS.

ON OPPOSITE SIDES ARE MANDELA AND BUTHELEZI, THE QUEEN CAN BE WINNIE, THE BISHOP CAN BE TUTU... AND OVER HERE IS ZULU KING ZWELITHINI.

GO AHEAD. IT'S YOUR MOVE.

WELL?! WHAT ARE YOU WAITING FOR?

INTERNATIONAL MEDIATION.

...FIRST TRIP IN A MINIBUS TAXI?

HOW'D YOU KNOW?

LIBRARY

CAN I HELP YOU?

YES. I'M LOOKING TO TAKE OUT A HUMOROUS BOOK.

SILENCE

...AN EXTREMELY FUNNY SATIRE THAT WILL CHALLENGE MY INTELLIGENCE AND MAKE ME ROAR WITH LAUGHTER.

HERE YOU GO.

WHAT IS IT?

"VOTING INSTRUCTIONS FOR THE LOCAL ELECTIONS."

147

LOOK AT THIS, MADAM... "DIRTY TRICK SQUADS" HAVE BEEN OPERATING SECRETLY IN THIS COUNTRY FOR YEARS!!

WE'RE NOT AFRAID OF DIRTY TRICKS, ARE WE MADAM?!

THAT'S RIGHT, EVE. NOBODY SILENCES US WHEN WE HAVE SOMETHING TO SAY!

IN FACT, LET'S TELL EVERYONE WHO IN THE GOVERNMENT IS INVOLVED.

GOOD IDEA. IT WAS

ALSO WE HAVE PROOF THAT THEY ARE

THE FACTS ARE CLEAR, EVE. SOMEONE'S SABOTAGING OUR CARTOON.

WE'RE VICTIMS OF A "DIRTY TRICKS" CAMPAIGN.

You're fired!

you CAN'T FIRE Me! I QuiT!

I DIDN'T SAY THAT.

NEITHER DID I. SOMEONE'S PUTTING WORDS IN OUR MOUTHS!

THIS IS SERIOUS, EVE.

you CAN saY THat aGaiN, Bone HEAD

EVE AND I HAVE AN IMPORTANT ANNOUNCEMENT: A DIRTY TRICKS SQUAD HAS SABOTAGED OUR CARTOON STRIP. THEREFORE, WE ARE NOT RESPONSIBLE FOR MAssAge pARlourS

AHEM... WE'RE NOT RESPONSIBLE FOR ThiRD FORCe ACtivity.

...WE'RE NOT RESPONSIBLE FOR... ANYTHING WE SAY OR DO!

WHEW. THANKS, EVE.

Don't MENTioN it, bird bRAiN.

I HEREBY CALL THE SECOND ANNUAL REUNION OF THE SECRET DIRTY TRICKS SQUADS TO ORDER!

BANG!

BLAM!

VERY FUNNY. AN EXPLODING GAVEL.

HEE-HEE!

CHUCKLE!

HEE-HEE!

© Rapid Phase Entertainment—1995

2nd ANNUAL DIRTY TRICKS SQUADS REUNION

...BOB?!

PIET! HOW HAVE YOU BEEN?!

WELL ACTUALLY, I'VE..I'VE...

FIRE! FIRE IN THE HOTEL!!

MADE YOU LOOK!

YOU'VE STILL GOT IT.

© Rapid Phase Entertainment—1995

2ND ANNUAL DIRTY TRICK SQUADS REUNION

ONE MORE QUESTION, MISTER X.

MAKE IT QUICK. THE FESTIVITIES ARE STARTING.

DO YOU REGRET THE DIRTY TRICKS CAMPAIGN YOU UNLEASHED UPON AN UNSUSPECTING PUBLIC?

REGRET?! WHY, WE'RE PROUD OF WHAT WE DID. PROUD!!

WOULD YOU MIND IF I TAKE YOUR PICTURE?

NO PROBLEM! GATHER ROUND, BOYS! GROUP PHOTO FOR THE NEWS-PAPERS!

© Rapid Phase Entertainment—1995

OKAY... SAY "CHEESE."

CHEESE.

I'M REPORTING LIVE FROM A DOWNTOWN HOTEL WHERE THE SECRET DIRTY TRICKS SQUADS ARE HOLDING THEIR SECOND ANNUAL **REUNION**.

...WHERE HUNDREDS OF DIRTY TRICKSTERS WILL BE TALKING OVER OLD TIMES AND PARTICIPATING IN AN AWARDS CEREMONY FOR "DIRTY TRICK OF THE YEAR."

CHUCKLE HEEHEE!

ALSO, IT'S RUMOURED THAT...

CHUCKLE
HEE-HEE!
HAHA!
HAHAHA!
HOOHOO!
HEE-HEE!

OKAY! WHAT'S SO **FUNNY**?!

KICK ME

AND WE'RE BACK WITH MORE LIVE COVERAGE OF THE SECOND ANNUAL REUNION OF THE SECRET DIRTY TRICKS SQUADS.

TELL ME, MISTER X. WHAT'S THE ONE THING YOUR MEMBERS HAVE IN COMMON?

SIMPLE. WE ALL LOVE A GOOD, HARMLESS PRACTICAL JOKE.

PRACTICAL JOKE?!! MANY OF THESE DIRTY TRICKS WEREN'T "JOKES"! THEY WERE DEVIOUS, VIOLENT--AND OFTEN RUINED PEOPLE'S LIVES!!

©Rupert Pearce Entertainment - 1995

MEDIA.

ABSOLUTELY NO SENSE OF HUMOUR.

MADAM & EVE

BY S. FRANCIS, H. DUGMORE & RICO

HI. I'M LOOKING FOR THE SECOND ANNUAL REUNION OF *DIRTY TRICKS* SQUAD MEMBERS.

NAME PLEASE?

MISTER X.

WE'VE HAD A *LOT* OF THOSE TONIGHT.

2ND ANNUAL DIRTY TRICKS SQUADS REUNION

THOSE WERE THE DAYS, MY FRIEND.

WE THOUGHT THEY'D NEVER END.

REMEMBER THE TIME WE RUINED THAT SINGER'S CAREER BY PUTTING TEAR GAS IN THE AIR CONDITIONING?

THAT WAS *YOU*?!!

WHAT ABOUT THE TELEPHONE BUGS?! ...THE FORGED CHEQUES!

≟CHUCKLE≟ AND THE SUIT TREATED WITH CHEMICALS WE SENT TO THAT GUY?!

≟SIGH≟   ≟SIGH≟

THERE'S NOTHING LIKE A GOOD DIRTY TRICK.

GOOD. BECAUSE I PUT A CHOCOLATE ECLAIR ON YOUR CHAIR. YOU'RE SITTING ON IT.

©Rapid Phase Entertainment - 1995

BY THE WAY... ENJOYING THAT CIGAR I GAVE YOU?

BLAM!

MEMORIES!

152

MADAM & Eve

BY S. FRANCIS, H. DUGMORE & RICO

MADAM! LOOK OUT!

CRASH! **24**

IT'S ONE OF THOSE EXTRA LARGE MAIL & GUARDIAN PAGE NUMBERS.

THOSE THINGS ARE DEADLY IF THEY FALL OFF THE TOP OF THE PAGE.

LOOK MADAM! THE SHOCK-WAVES OPENED UP A HOLE IN THE SPACE-TIME CARTOON-STRIP CONTINUUM.

YOU MEAN...

YES! WE CAN LEAVE! WE'RE FREE! FREE FROM THE BOUNDARIES OF PEN & INK!

FREE TO EXPLORE NEW WORLDS... TO BOLDLY GO WHERE NO OTHER CARTOON CHARACTERS HAVE GONE BEFORE -- INTO THE REST OF THE NEWSPAPER.

EXCEPT FOR ONE PROBLEM.

THAT GRANDIOSE SPEECH YOU JUST MADE TOOK UP TWO PANELS... AND NOW THE HOLE IS WAY UP THERE.

THE LAWS OF CARTOON PHYSICS ARE TRULY AMAZING.

BUT HEY-- NO PROBLEM! ALL THE PANELS ARE WEAK... SEE?

COME. LET'S GO!

WAIT FOR ME!

EVE! I FOUND THIS BURIED BY MY ROSES. WHAT DO YOU THINK IT IS?

OFF HAND, I'D SAY THAT'S A FOSSILIZED HUMAN FOOT BONE OVER 3.5 MILLION YEARS OLD AND PROVING CONCLUSIVELY THAT EARLY MAN EVOLVED ON THIS CONTINENT.

WHY DO THESE THINGS ALWAYS END UP IN MY GARDEN?

MADAM -- THAT FOSSILIZED BONE YOU JUST THREW AWAY IS AN ARCHEOLOGICAL FIND! IT COULD BE WORTH MILLIONS!

GRRR...

SCREECH!

NICE DOGGIE.

LOOK ON THE BRIGHT SIDE. HE'LL HAVE TO DROP THE BONE TO EAT US.

KEEP DIGGING, EVE! WE ALREADY UNEARTHED ONE VALUABLE FOSSIL... THERE'S NO TELLING WHAT ELSE WE'LL FIND HIDDEN IN THE EARTH!

MADAM! THERE'S SOMETHING BURIED DOWN HERE!

CLUNK!

WHAT IS IT?

TINS OF BEANS... AND CANDLES

...PRE-HISTORIC MAN?

PRE-ELECTION MAN.

MADAM & Eve

BY S. FRANCIS, H. DUGMORE & RICO

...AND IN OTHER NEWS... A FOSSILIZED FOOT BONE WAS DISCOVERD TODAY, PROVING THAT A HUMAN FAMILY LIVED NEAR JOHANNESBURG OVER 3,5 MILLION YEARS AGO...

EVE! HAVE YOU FINISHED IRONING THE BEARSKINS YET?!

EVE! THE BIG BALL OF FIRE IN THE SKY IS GOING DOWN! WHERE'S MY GYPSUM AND TONIC?!

I'M DOING THE BEST I CAN! I ONLY HAVE TWO OPPOSABLE THUMBS!

EVE! IT'S GETTING LATE! WHAT'S FOR DINNER?

YOUR FAVOURITE. KENTUCKY FRIED PTERODACTYL.

GOOD. I'M STARVED.

EASY FOR YOU TWO TO SAY. ALL YOU DO IS SIT IN FRONT OF THE CAVE PAINTINGS ALL DAY.

CRASH!

AAAH!? WHAT ARE THEY DOING HERE?!

HOO! HOO! HOO! HOO! HOO! HOO!

DON'T TELL ME YOU ACCIDENTALLY PUSHED THE ARMED RESPONSE BUTTON AGAIN?!

SORRY MADAM.

HOO HOO HOO HOO

HOO HOO

POP!

WHEW! WHAT A NIGHTMARE.

EVE! STOP LYING AROUND AND CLEAN UP! THIS PLACE IS STARTING TO LOOK LIKE A CAVE!!

©Rapid Phase Entertainment - 1995

MADAM & Eve

BY S. FRANCIS, H. DUGMORE & RICO

HI GRANDMA. THIS IS MY FRIEND BOB. HE'S A HOMEOPATH.

GWEN!!

I'M RIGHT HERE, MOM. WHAT'S WRONG?

IT'S ERIC! HE'S SPENDING TIME WITH... A... HOMEOPATH!

OH. YOU MEAN BOB.

YOU MEAN, YOU APPROVE?!

OF COURSE! BOB'S VERY TALENTED. I HOPE SOME OF HIS QUALITIES RUB OFF ON ERIC.

YOU MEAN, YOU ACTUALLY WANT ERIC TO BECOME A ...HOMEOPATH?!

I'D BE VERY HAPPY. BUT I WON'T PUSH HIM. IT'S HIS DECISION.

MOM... A "HOMEOPATH" IS LIKE A DOCTOR. A SPECIALIST IN NATURAL MEDICINE.

OH.

SO BOB HAS A GIRLFRIEND.

I DOUBT IT. HE'S GAY.

163

GOOD MORNING GAUTENG!

THIS IS YOUR NEW DJ SWINGIN' TOKYO SEXWALE... THE MAN WITH THE PLAN... THE PREMIER WITHOUT FEAR...AND NEW DUDE ON YOUR RADIO BLOCK!!

IN A MOMENT, I'LL BE RAPPIN' AND CHATTIN'... GROOVIN' AND MOVIN'... BUT FIRST-- HERE'S A BLAST FROM THE PAST! "YMCA"...BY THE VILLAGE PEOPLE! THIS ONE GOES OUT TO YOU, MADIBA!!

©Rapid Phase Entertainment - 1995

♫ IT'S FUN TO STAY AT THE... Y.M.C.A!! ♫

I DIDN'T KNOW YOU LIKED THE VILLAGE PEOPLE, SIR.

GROAN!

...HELLO, TOKYO?

GO AHEAD, M'MAN. YOU'RE ON THE AIR.

TOKYO... I JUST WANT TO SAY THAT YOU'RE DOING A GREAT JOB AS A DJ.

THANKS, DUDE. AND I WANT TO STRESS, I'M HERE AS AN UNBIASED PRESENTER, NOT AS AN OFFICIAL OF THE ANC.

GOOD. BECAUSE I HAVE A QUESTION. DO YOU THINK THE FAILURE OF THE RDP IS DUE TO...

CLICK

OOPS.

©Rapid Phase Entertainment - 1995

TOKYO-- THAT'S THE FIFTH CALLER YOU CUT OFF!

AN ACCIDENT! I SWEAR!

ALRIGHT! THIS IS SWINGIN' TOKYO SEXWALE-- THE MIDNIGHT RAMBLER! LET'S RAP. HELLO--YOU'RE ON THE AIR.

HELLO, MISTER SEXWALE. WHAT TIME DOES THE NEXT GRAVY TRAIN LEAVE?

THE WHAT?

THE GRAVY TRAIN! THE ONE YOU AND ALL THE OTHER ANC OFFICIALS ARE RIDING ON!

WHERE'S ALL THE FREE HOUSING YOU PROMISED?! AND THE CRIME RATE-- FORGET ABOUT IT! AND ANOTHER THING--

WAIT A MINUTE. YOU SOUND FAMILIAR! WHO IS THIS?!

©Rapid Phase Entertainment - 1995

MISTER LEON, THE MEETING'S STARTING.

SHH! CAN'T YOU SEE I'M ON THE TELEPHONE?

DP

MADAM & Eve

BY S. FRANCIS, H. DUGMORE & RICO

HELLO? WHO'S CALLING?

MRS. VERWOERD?

WHAT A COINCIDENCE, THAT'S MY NAME TOO!

NO, MRS. VERWOERD, THIS IS MRS. ANDERSON. I WANT TO TALK ABOUT **NELSON MANDELA**.

I'M SORRY, DEAR. HE'S NOT HERE. HE LEFT LONG AGO.

NO... MRS. VERWOERD. I'VE BEEN NOTIFIED THAT THE PRESIDENT WILL VISIT ME NEXT AS PART OF HIS **T.C.E.W.** PROGRAM.

T.C.E.W.?

TEA WITH CONSERVATIVE ELDERLY WHITE WOMEN.

I SEE.

ANYWAY... WHEN MR MANDELA ARRIVES, I WAS WONDERING IF YOU COULD TELL ME WHAT TO EXPECT.

WELL, FIRST OF ALL, HE'S BLACK...

YES MRS. VERWOERD, I KNOW THAT.

...AND WHATEVER YOU DO, DON'T STARE AT HIS SHIRT! YOU'LL GET DIZZY.

ALSO, HE TRAVELS WITH **LOTS** OF PEOPLE. LOCK THE BATHROOM.

MRS VERWOERD, WHAT WOULD YOU SAY WAS THE **MOST MEMORABLE** PART OF HIS VISIT?

NOTHING WAS MISSING AFTER THEY LEFT.

WHO WAS THAT, MOM?

WRONG NUMBER.

© Rapid Phase Entertainment – 1995

169

Dear Mister President, Thank you for having tea with my friend mother Anderson.

It was very special because she usually does not have tea with very many black people.

Also, she usually drinks gin instead of tea. Maybe you could bring some next time. Your friend thandi.

WELL? WHAT DO YOU THINK?

NEEDS WORK.

©Rapid Phase Entertainment - 1995

MISTER PRESIDENT--THERE'S OVER TWO HUNDRED ELDERLY CONSERVATIVE WHITE WOMEN IN A QUEUE DOWNSTAIRS!

WHAT?! WHAT DO THEY WANT?!

WELL, ACTUALLY SIR... THEY ALL WANT TO HAVE TEA WITH YOU.

...I STARTED A TREND, DIDN'T I?

AFRAID SO, SIR.

©Rapid Phase Entertainment - 1995

...I'M NINETY-TWO, I LIKE COOKING, SEWING AND I SUPPORT THE VOLKSTAAT.

HAVE A SEAT AND FILL OUT THIS APPLICATION FORM.

MADAM & Eve

BY S. FRANCIS, H. DUGMORE & RICO

PRESENTING: EVE... AND THE MADAMETTES!

WAIT!

OH YEAH! WAIT A MINUTE MISTER POSTMAN!

PLEASE MISTER POSTMAN-- LOOK AND SEE...

...IS THERE A LETTER IN YOUR BAG FOR ME...?

I'VE BEEN STANDIN' HERE WAITIN' MISTER POSTMAN--

SO WHOAH WHOAH PATIENTLY...

FOR JUST A CARD OR JUST A LETTER...

PLEASE CHECK IT AND SEE-- JUST ONE MORE TIME FOR ME--

PLEASE MISTER POST-MAN!

DELIVER DE LETTER... DE SOONER DE BETTER...

...YOU GOTTA WAIT A MINUTE, WAIT A MINUTE -- OH YEAH!! WAIT A MINUTE... PLEASE MISTER POSTMAN...

MADAM & Eve

BY S.FRANCIS, H.DUGMORE & RICO.

A **TOAST** TO THE GOVERNMENT OF NATIONAL UNITY! A YEAR OF **FREEDOM**, **EQUALITY** AND POSITIVE CHANGES!

CHEERS! HEAR! HEAR!

MADAM! COME QUICKLY! YOU LEFT THE HANDBRAKE OFF ON YOUR **NEW** BMW!

UH-OH.

BUMP BUMP BUMP BU

SCREECH!

WELL, IT'S ABOUT TIME.